Life in Ethiopia

by Job K. Savage

AuthorHouse™
1663 Liberty Drive
Bloomington, IN 47403
www.authorhouse.com
Phone: 1-800-839-8640

First published by AuthorHouse 8/26/2010

ISBN: 978-1-4520-5269-4 (sc)
ISBN: 978-1-4520-5268-7 (e)

Printed in the United States of America

This book is printed on acid-free paper.

On the Cover:

Emperor Haile Selassie bidding French President, Georges Pompidou, fairwell in 1973 following a state visit. The event took place at the international airport in Addis Ababa. My wife and I were present for the ceremony. Never will forget the ramrod stance of Haile Selassie and how he held that stance while Pompidou delivered his rather lengthy remarks. Photo from book titled "Ethiopie", photo credited to photographer Bernard Gerard.

Acknowledgments

First, I want to thank the authors of those publications listed in the Bibliography for making it possible for me to write this book. I have endeavored to give them credit for any of their material that I have used.

Second, I wish to make it clear that I have only selected those portions of Ethiopian history that I consider worthy of consideration as a historical highlight (outstanding, unique, and interesting). Undoubtedly there are some historical events worthy of inclusion that are missing, and some included that readers think should not have been. I accept responsibility for both. I also accept complete responsibility for any transfer errors of fact.

Many thanks to Linda Somberg for her valuable help in formatting the manuscript and in putting the text into a uniform typed document. She inserted many of the pictures and other graphics, and was responsible for dealing with the publisher's staff responsible for printing the book. To summarize, I could not have done it without her.

I wish to thank the staff of Author House Publishing, particular those (add names) who have reviewed the manuscript and made it more readable and to those concerned with sale of the book. Also I wish to thank Author House who has so ably served as my author advocate.

Finally I wish to thank my wife for excusing me from some of my household chores at various times that I might devote time to writing the book.

Table of Contents

Table of Contents

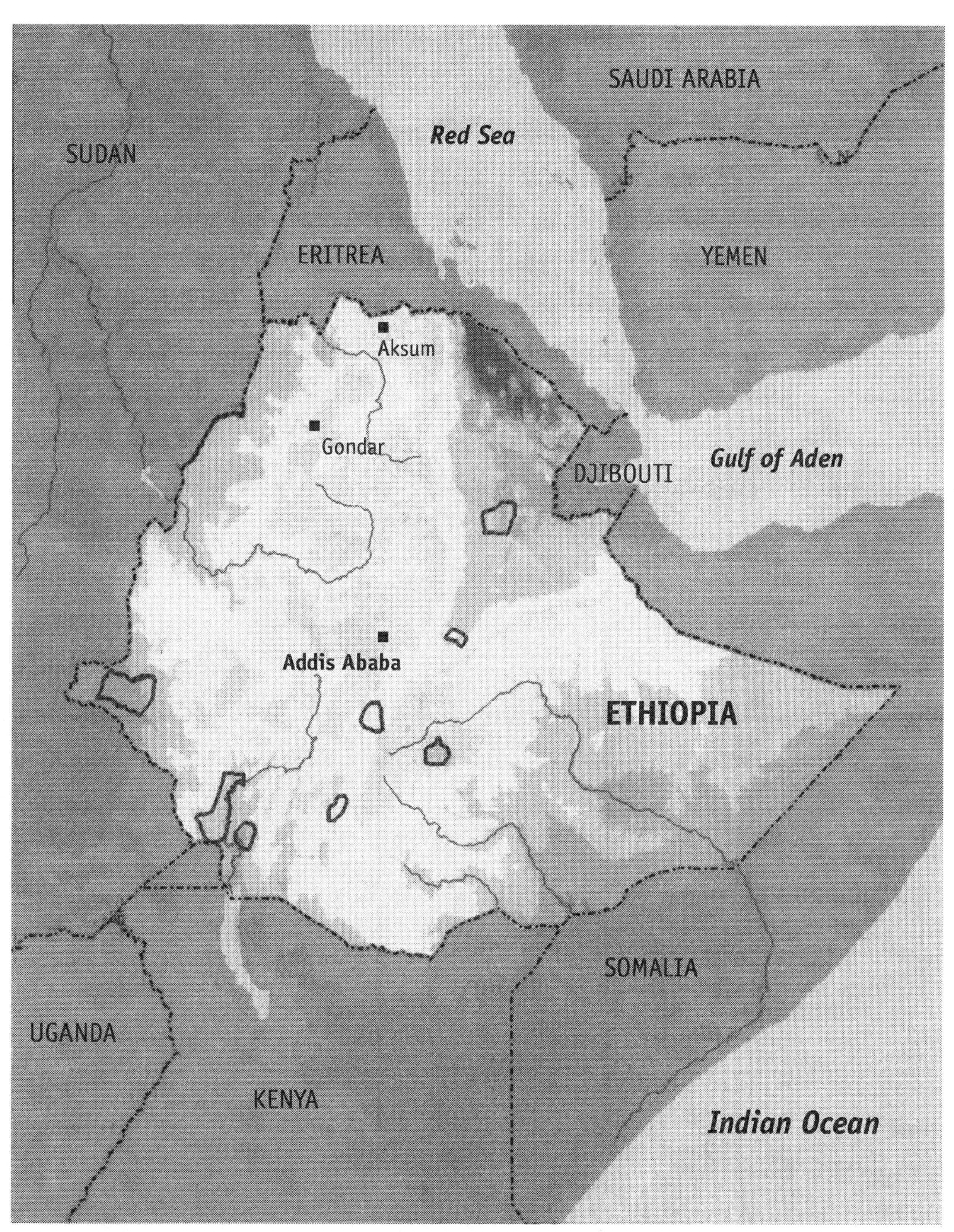
SAUDI ARABIA
Red Sea
SUDAN
ERITREA
YEMEN
Aksum
Gondar
DJIBOUTI
Gulf of Aden
Addis Ababa
ETHIOPIA
SOMALIA
UGANDA
KENYA
Indian Ocean

Introduction

I would like to explain how this book came to pass. Please bear with me for a few pages about living in Ethiopia before we come to how this unique ad unusual country began. As with many things in one's life, it was not exactly planned... it just happened. Looking back, it actually began when I resigned my job with the US Department of Agriculture in Washington, DC. After some thirty plus years, I decided take a job with the Ministry of Agriculture in Ethiopia.

My wife and I have had the good fortune of spending time in a number of African countries – east, west, north, and south – including two years in Ethiopia. Of all these countries, Ethiopia has fascinated us the most. It is the oldest and blessed with a written history that reaches back about two thousand years. We were taken in by its many interesting and different people, the history, government, agriculture, religions, churches, cathedrals, monasteries, myths, mix of civilizations, and customs. According to some of those most familiar with Ethiopia's history, it is believed to be the birthplace of some of the earliest humans.

While we were there I was busy working. I did not have time to learn very much about the details of the aforementioned items, but as the years rolled by I never forgot Ethiopia. Of course people, knowing that we had lived there, would frequently ask us what it was like. When we lived in Williamsburg, VA the Christopher Wren Association asked me to teach a short course on Ethiopia. I agreed, and it was then that I had to do some rather intense studying in order to teach a class that was in large part made up of senior citizen professionals. Now that I am no longer engaged in my profession as an Economist and have some time for other activities, I have decided to share with you some of the uniqueness of this special country.

Ethiopia lived up to our expectations and more. Now some thirty five years later, I thought why not acquaint you with some of our experiences in that country and the knowledge we have gained from living over there? And perhaps more important, I want to share what I have learned from studying the history of that country. I write now with more than twenty years of work experience in twelve other African countries, as well as other countries throughout the world. Looking back, I was a bit naïve about how foreign countries operate and the problems they had. In addition, I have had a number of opportunities to get better acquainted with Ethiopia through teaching about it and presenting numerous talks about this country. Had I this experience when I was in Ethiopia during its crisis period of 1972-74, it would have been helpful in writing this book, but one must do the best one can with what is available to them at the time.

Before getting into the major highlights of this story, I would like to share with you what it's like moving to a foreign country thousands of miles from your home, and having to settle in to new surroundings. It is a complicated process, and someone not experienced in these matters just has to learn by going through it, and hope for the best.

In early January, 1972 I gave Eric Thor, head of Farmer Cooperative Service, notice that I would be retiring in February and going to work in Ethiopia in March. He did not try to dissuade me. Actually, I am sure he had someone he wanted to take my place. Thor had been appointed by the Nixon Administration some months after it took office in 1971. It had taken a while for the Nixon Administration to decide on a successor to David Angevine who had previously headed the agency. I was not pleased with Thor's appointment or the way he ran the agency. I did not consider that he knew very much about cooperatives since his working experience was elsewhere, but he had supported Nixon in the political campaign that put him in office. As the saying goes, "to the victor go the spoils." On a personal basis I did not dislike him, we just had different philosophies.

The next few weeks were busy for me, cleaning up all the loose ends – including my desk and files. I was also reading all the material I could get my hands on about Ethiopia. I was busy asking people in the department who had been to Ethiopia or had some knowledge of that country what it was like. I found it all very interesting, especially Haile Selassie, the ruler or benevolent dictator, as some described him. I was excited at the prospects of living over there and already thinking that it seemed like a different country than many of the other African countries I had heard about.

This was especially true when some of my sources would mention that Ethiopia was said to be the oldest Christian Empire in the world, or that it had a written language before Christ called Ge'ez. There was mention made that it was a dynasty and had nobility like Western Europe. These bits of information certainly perked my interest and I resolved to learn more about these exciting developments. I even heard that some scientists thought human civilization may have begun here. Of course my assignment did not include learning about these events. It was years after I left Ethiopia that circumstances led me to find out more about these and other interesting bits of history of this unusual country.

The day finally arrived in early March of 1972 when we left our home in Crofton, MD. We boarded the plane at Dulles Airport for our trip to begin my two year Ethiopian assignment. January and February of that year had been exciting months for Agnes and me. And yet somewhat sad. I had enjoyed my work with the Department, and had many friends that I would miss. Some that I would probably never see again. I was given a couple of retirement parties, one by the Department and one by my agency. Of course the saddest thing that happened was my father's death. He died the day before I was honored by my agency at a lovely party in a posh restaurant in Virginia. I did not want to put a damper on the party, so I never mentioned his passing at the party.

Our route to Ethiopia was by way of London for a two day rest and sightseeing stop. Agnes and I had been to London on our 25th wedding anniversary in 1963. I had also been there during WWII, and on working trips while I was in the Department of Agriculture. Because we had already seen so much of London we spent a good deal of our time resting and eating. We did not fly directly from London Heathrow Airport to Ethiopia, but were routed by Rome. It was nearly midnight when we were finally underway, and we made one stop somewhere in Africa before we finally landed in Addis Ababa, Ethiopia the next day. We had a hotel reservation in the heart of the city at a good – but not best – hotel in the city. I no longer recall the name, but it was to be our home for the next two weeks until we could locate permanent quarters. We later learned that the Ethiopian Hilton Hotel was the best hotel, and there was another older hotel, likely owned by someone in Haile Sellassie's family, that was also considered to be very good.

After we had a night's sleep and were somewhat rested, I called Layne Holdcroft, my contact with USAID in Addis. Layne was head of the agricultural sector in USAID. He was most kind and helpful to us. He and his charming wife invited us to a get together at his home. When we arrived, he had gathered some of his key staff to meet and to advise us about how to get started in the settling in process. Not much was said about what I would be doing at this time. That would come later after we had located a place to live and acquired some furniture, appliances and other living necessities. Our contractor, Trans Century, had allowed us to ship 300 pounds of household items as part of our contract. This was quickly used up to bring linens, extra clothing, and cooking utensils. One of the cooking utensils was a pressure cooker, and was probably the most useful item we brought. I will never forget that cooker!

As one can imagine, our work was cut out for us, and especially for Agnes. Our first move after the session at Layne's house was to decide where we would live and find such a place. We realized we could do little until we had a place to live. It had been pointed out to us that there were houses that could be rented in what was known as the American compound, or ghetto. This was an area in Addis where most American employees of the American Embassy and other related institutions lived. After some thought, we decided we would prefer to live somewhere other than the American compound. I believe our decision was more of a hunch at the time than one backed by lengthy reasoning. In any event, we came to see later that we had made a good decision. Had we opted for a house it would have been necessary to hire Sabanyas (guards) on a 24-hour basis to guard our house. Houses in Addis occupied by foreigners and Ethiopians who could afford to do so were all fenced and guarded by Saybanas. Most of the homes also had dogs. I always thought the dogs were necessary to make sure the guards stayed awake, especially at night. This arrangement was not necessary if we rented an apartment, and so we decided on an apartment. We were able to locate one very near where I would be working – in fact so close I walked to work most of the time.

Palace gate of Haile Selassi's main palace in Addis Ababa.

The apartment was about three blocks from Haile Sellassie's palace where he resided most of the time. The houses in our area were not overly elegant. It was a mixed area, some good and some not so good. The apartment belonged to an Italian firm, Sellcoast, and was well kept and run. We had one bedroom, two baths, a large living room with a sizeable space for dining, and a good sized kitchen. The apartment was located on the second floor. There was a fireplace in the living room, but we were warned not to try to use it because it was unsafe. The apartment was completely unfurnished, so Agnes and I set about to make up a list of furniture and appliances we would need. We would also need a maid to cook and keep house.

Needless to say the list was not difficult to make, but filling it was not easy. There were no stores selling ready made furniture. We were able to locate people who hand-made furniture and would take orders to fill them rather promptly. Our first items were bed, chairs, tables, and a sleep sofa. Then we turned to the kitchen where we needed a stove and refrigerator. Fortunately, we were able to find a store that stocked these items. I seem to recall it carried Phillip's electrical appliances. Of course we also needed lamps, and they were available. As mentioned, we had brought a few cooking items and more were available at the market.

With many of our household items arranged, our thoughts turned to transportation – an automobile. For the first day or so in Addis, we had relied on taxis to get us around. Then we began to look for auto dealers, and surprise...we found there were a few. Of course the Japanese had cars for sale, at least the Nissan Company that makes the Datsun was there. We would be able to get a new Datsun in about two weeks. What really clinched the deal was that the local dealer had a used car we could drive until our new one arrived. We drove it away. The car was larger than the one we had ordered. In fact it was the top of the line made by Nissan. It was plush, but it was not a very new model. In any event, it carried us around until the new one arrived about two weeks later.

With some of the more pressing items taken care of we decided to ride around the city and see some sights. We saw churches, statues, homes of the well-to-do, the zoo that contained Haile Sellassie's famous lions, and the headquarters of the Organization of African Unity. Of course at this time we often did not know what we were looking at, but it was interesting and new to us. Of particular note to us was the octagon-shaped Saint George Coptic Christian Cathedral that we later learned was built in 1896. We enjoyed our short tour and promised ourselves that we would do more, but now we had more pressing business to take care.

After about ten days we had assembled enough furniture and a maid, and could move from the hotel to our apartment. I should mention that our maid was Tetalesh, who had previously worked for an English couple and had learned to speak very passable English. This was very fortunate, since we spoke no Amharic at that time. We did not realize it at the time, but we were apparently setting a record for getting settled in and ready to report for work. In two weeks time after arriving in the country, I reported to the Ministry of Agriculture for duty. My counterpart was surprised. He expected me to show up about a month after arrival. The credit for this goes to my wife Agnes who had organized the settling in process. Of course not all the settling in had been completed, but enough that we could move in and I could go to work.

Headquarters of Organization of African Unity located in Addis Ababa.

Getting Down to Work

The first day or so on the job was devoted to getting to meet some of the people I would be working with. My counterpart was a young man who had a B.S. Degree in Agricultural Economics from Iowa State University. He headed a section titled Economic Development, as best I can recall. There was at least one other professional in the section who had attended college in the U.S. and who had a degree from one of our agricultural universities. There were one or two secretaries, and a typist in the section. They all spoke English and were very pleasant. I was assigned a desk and office space and went to work. I had a private office, but it was certainly not in a class with the one I occupied in Farmer Cooperative Service. After all I was now working in a third world country – and one of the poorest at that.

Agnes and Tetalesh were busy locating additional furnishings for the apartment and cooking and cleaning up. All seemed to be going well. After we had been in the apartment for a few days, Agnes began to notice a car parked on the street just below our balcony during the day with a man sitting in it. This seemed to be a daily routine. About this same time, anytime Agnes would get a telephone call from some friends, it sounded as though someone else was listening to her conversation. We thought about this situation for a day or so and concluded we were being checked out by the Ethiopian intelligence service. I do not know the actual name of this service, but I had heard such a service existed. It did seem reasonable that Haile Selassie would employ such a service. We had been warned to be careful about what we said about him or how the country was run by him. Much of the local paper was devoted to favorable activities associated with the Emperor. Most of the foreigners referred to him as Mr. Smith. Agnes is a lady of action, so one day after having her conversation interrupted by someone listening on the line she went to the telephone exchange and demanded to talk to the person in charge. She was actually allowed to do so. When a man showed up and wanted to know what she wanted, Agnes let him know she was much annoyed by having her conversation interfered with by some of his personnel. She told him she did not care if she was listened to as long as she was not interrupted. It must have worked, because the monitored telephone conversations ceased, and the man sitting in the car outside our apartment disappeared.

I had an idea before leaving Washington as to what my first work would be. Put simply, USAID wanted me to develop a method that could be used by the heads of agricultural sections in Ethiopia. To gather evaluating data on the projects being financed with USAID funds. The data would then be turned over to other professionals to analyze and determine how well the projects were progressing. It was a neat idea if it could be made to work. I had some ideas, and early on was assigned to go to work on it. After about three months I developed a method whereby the project leaders could gather the data necessary to evaluate the progress of the projects. It also included the data for establishing a base line necessary for a proper evaluation.

In a meeting I presented the plan to the top staff in the Ministry, including the Minister, and it was accepted. Unfortunately, when the plan was given to the project leaders, they never carried through. They were not going to put themselves in a position where they might have to report their project as being in trouble, and those in a position to enforce the order were not of a mind to do so. I also think some of these project leaders considered this tracking work to be superfluous. Looking back, maybe the idea was not so good after all? It did put the project leaders in a position of having to possibly condemn themselves, and their superiors also might have had to bear some of the blame. We should have realized this would happen and not begun the plan, but we did not have the advantage of hindsight. The plan was in place for awhile but not much ever happened so it just died a slow death. I quickly became engaged on other projects, such as assisting in preparing the Ministry budget. I had some experience in budget preparation and presentation due to similar work I had done in Farmer Cooperative Service.

Another of my duties from time to time was to represent my section in numerous meetings that were attended by other Ministries of the Ethiopian government. Often there were representatives from numerous other countries attending these meetings. Ethiopia had sought development help from a number of countries and many of them had responded favorably. Some that I recall besides the US were England, France, Norway, Sweden, and Germany. And from the East there were Chinese and Russians. Also I seem to recall there were some Bulgarians. Bulgaria at that time was operating under a Communistic form of government, as were the Chinese and Russians. I did not realize it then, but the Communist Party was sowing the seeds that would bear fruit in the coming years. Even the Cubans would come in. There were meetings then when five year plans were discussed. I believe this was my first exposure to such plans. I had heard of such plans, but had always associated them with Communistic countries. To the best of my knowledge, none of these plans were ever adopted while I was in Ethiopia.

Sufficient to say, I was usefully employed during my two-year period and was asked to return for another two-year period, but declined. Agnes and I planned to get back to the U.S. and experience some of the pleasures of retirement. While we were in Ethiopia, the major topic of some of our conversations was what we would do when we returned home. And yes, we would discuss how we would return home. More about this later.

Living Conditions in Ethiopia

We are often asked what it was like to live in a country such as Ethiopia. One of the things that stand out in our mind is the abject poverty that exists all around. It is exemplified in so many aspects of living. One example was the beggars all around you on the streets and at any place where there was a crowd, such as at church. I recall that the beggars would completely surround our car when went to church on Sunday at eleven in the morning. It made it very difficult for us to get out of our car. Because of this, we changed our church hour to the early service at eight in the morning. This helped. Then at night when you were returning from a party or some other event, at any street corner where one had to stop, a young child would approach your car with hands outstretched – begging. It was pitiful, but we soon learned that whatever you gave to them would be taken from them by their handler who was standing on side of the street just waiting to take from them what you had given. Instead of giving, you had to speak harshly to them in language they understood. This made us feel guilty and bad.

You would also see old women carrying bundles of sticks on their backs or carrying heavy jugs of water on their heads. Seeing this made you think these people had never heard the wheel had been invented. They did not have water in their homes, and the sticks were for the little hibachis they cooked on. Gas or electric stoves were too expensive for them. Since the vast majority of the population were too poor to afford them, the country was being rapidly stripped of the forests. The forests were important in preventing erosion that washed away the topsoil and further impoverished the country. It also used up the forests that were needed to provide the country with timber for building homes and other facilities. The tragedy is that this poverty was not necessary. It was the result of a faulty political system that had not allowed the masses of people to use the resources of the country to produce a much larger gross product. It was one that could be distributed on a more equitable basis to those who could have made it possible to bring the increase about. Of course we were not aware that at this time activities were underway to revamp the political system and the control of the country. Both of these would help these poor people.

Fortunately, there was more than poverty and misery to be seen and experienced in Ethiopia. To mention some of the pleasant offsets – there were churches, public buildings, and homes ranging from round thatch covered huts to unique styled mansions. There were people dressed in anything from Western styled clothes to native shamas (a dress resembling a sheet draped around the body, worn by men and women). Ethiopia's Ruler, Haile Selassie, was looked upon as one of the more important political leaders in Africa, and thus attracted several outstanding international buildings. These were somewhat unique and attracted people dressed in a variety of native costumes. This was interesting to see.

Also one must not forget the pleasant weather that Addis Ababa is blessed with year round – no heat or air conditioning required. And yes, the native food is different from that of any other country I have ever been in. WAT & INJERA is the food and TEJ & TALLOW are used to wash it down. Explanation: Watt is a large pancake made from a tiny indigenous cereal grain known as teff. The pancake is laden with a variety of foods depending upon the taste and financial status of the person(s) consuming it. It is a staple for Ethiopian families, and the food on the pancake depends on what the family can afford. Food includes such items as chicken, pork, mutton, lamb or goat, along with varieties of vegetables including beans. Tej is liquor made by letting honey ferment – right powerful. We liked it. The tallow is what we think of as home brew and most any food substance might be used to make it. We did not care for it. Fortunately, my wife and I are fond of Chinese food and there were at least three good Chinese restaurants in Addis.

The Italians had left their mark on the food situation, primarily the introduction of spaghetti. Of course we ate at home most of the time and Tetalesch, our maid, was a good cook. With some help from Agnes and the pressure cooker, we made out just fine. I must note that Agnes laid the law down to Tetalesch about water sanitation. All drinking water had to be boiled and strained, and there were to be no uncooked vegetables including salads. When we returned home and were examined by our doctor, there were no signs of disease or infection from our stay in Ethiopia. I will mention that Tetalesh taught me how to make good banana pancakes.

Agnes at the entrance to our apartment complex in Addis Ababa.

At night we often heard a strange howling like noise, almost human like, after we were in bed. After considerable discussion with several of the other tenants in our apartment building we learned that the noise

[1]A book that I had published in 02/24/05 by AuthorHouse titled "TARBORO TO KATMANDU" contains considerable information relevant to this book and liberal use will be made of that data here.

Hyena Creek, we called it, behind our apartment complex.

was coming from hyenas who frequented the creek running behind our building. Once we knew what it was, we were no longer disturbed by the hyenas.

It took us a bit longer to get used to the natives using the sidewalks, streets, and vacant lots to relieve themselves. In fact, I don't believe we ever did. Of course Ethiopia is not the only country that resorts to this practice, because they cannot afford indoor plumbing. It so happened that there was a vacant lot just across the street from our apartment and we named it Tinkle Park. I must say that the odor during the very dry season was not pleasant.

Seeing Some of the Sights Outside Addis

At this time we had only been in Ethiopia a few months and there was much we had not seen or done. We began to think about where we would like to go. There were many choices to select from, especially since we had seen so little of the country at that time. It was not very difficult for me to get off from work to take short trips in the country. We decided to invite John Gammons, our god child and the grandson of Helen Spurzem, a close friend, to come over to visit us for a few weeks. He was 14 years old and we knew he would enjoy Ethiopia. His visit would also enable us to get to see some of the country that we had heard about but not seen.

Agnes standing in the entrance of an old palace in Gondar.

We flew by plane to Gondar and rented car with a driver for a few days to see the area in that part of Ethiopia. Gondar was a former capital of Ethiopia and was selected because it seemed to be a very interesting place and was also well located for other places that we planned to visit. It was at least 400 years old and still standing were several old castles built by emperors, nobles, and other high ranking officials. The first and most imposing of the palaces was that of Emperor Fasiladas and the last palace built there was that of Emperor Yasu II. Altogether there were 20 palaces in Gondar and surrounding area. Fasiladas founded the city of Gondar in 1636 and began constructing his palace soon thereafter.

According to historians, Gondar represented a return to a more tranquil life for the emperors. They were tired of living in military camps and constantly fighting as was the custom during much of Ethiopia's existence. The older capital at Axum represented a period when Ethiopia was at its zenith and was a highly respected dynasty in most of the civilized world. The advance of the Muslims had driven the Ethiopians out of Axum and into military camps for many years until their emperors became complacent and established a more permanent capital in Gondar.

After devoting a day or so looking over the sights in Gondar we had our driver take us to see the Falashans (Black Jews) who had settled in villages outside Gondar. In Ethiopia they ranked pretty low and lived in villages not up to the standards of other villages, or so it seemed to us, They eked out a living from making artifacts, especially from items prepared from iron heated in open fires and then shaped on anvils that resembled those of blacksmiths. These were some of the same Jews that later migrated to Israel.

The Blue Nile as it winds its way through a gorge in Ethiopia.

Ournextplaceofinterestwastosee Lake Tana, located on the edge of Gondar. This is a very large lake with many small islands, many of them inhabited by monks and churches. Also Lake Tana is the source of the Blue Nile river and we devoted a morning getting to a site just outside Gondar where one can view the lake spilling out water to a stream below the level of the lake as a waterfall would do. Some years later when I was in Uganda I was privileged to see the beginning of the White Nile as it comes from its primary source Lake Victoria.

That afternoon we boarded a small motor launch that would take us to a historical church on one of the islands in Lake Tana. Once there we were ushered into the church by the head priest who proudly escorted us through the church pointing out any unusual features of the church and reciting its long history. Also he showed us a large Ethiopian Cross and the colorful trappings surrounding it. I must say it was all most impressive and we expressed our appreciation by leaving a generous donation. It was now time to get aboard our motor launch and head back to Gondar.

Once aboard, a member of the crew began to crank the engine by hand using a piece of rope to turn the engine over. The engine failed to start, sputtering now and then enough to encourage us that it would surely start with the next pull of the rope, but no such luck. The cranking continued with another crew member spelling off the first one. It was beginning to get darker and it would soon be night fall and I could see no other means to travel back to Gondar. I had visions of spending the night in the church as there was no other place for us to stay as far as I knew. The cranking continued and much to our relief after about an hour of continuous cranking and sputtering the engine started and we all let out a cheer. On our way back I asked the captain what would have happened had the engine failed to start. He explained that if the boat did not arrive after a designated time another boat would be sent to pick us up. Our worries were over nothing. Of course no one thought to let us know this until I asked. In any event we were left with a good story to tell.

Wart hogs crossing a road in Ethiopia.

An Ethiopian priest displays a Bible, incense vessels and other colorful trappings from a nearby church on Lake Tana.

The beginning of the Blue Nile as it flows out of Lake Tana.

Lake Tana is the source of the Blue Nile. Several Rivers flow out of Lake Tana and combine to form the Blue Nile. The Tiss Issat Falls flowing with water from Lake Tana.

Falashans (black Jews) making metal artifacts.

Seeing Some of the Sights Outside Addis

Agnes is helping an Ethiopian child. This picture was taken to show that the plane had landed on a dirt runway – actually a muddy runway.

The next morning we boarded an Ethiopian Airlines plane, a DC 3 that would take us to the town of Lalibela and the famous stone churches there, known as the churches of Lalibela. They were named for the person responsible for their construction King Lalibela, who reigned from 1190 to 1225 AD. The churches were carved from solid rock and some of them are connected by tunnels carved from the rock.

Airport terminal at Lalibela.

We landed on a dirt runway and a muddy one at that. Needles to say we all were relieved when the plane skidded to a halt. I am sure this was the first time that any of us had landed in a DC 3 on a dirt runway. We were told later that the planes stopped landing here when the rainy season begins, which was about now. In fact it had already arrived as the runway was already muddy. We were met by a jeep that passed as a taxi and taken up the side of a mountain to very poor excuse for a hotel that was owned by a member of the royal family we learned later.

For about two days we explored the old churches with some of the priests serving as guides. John was invited to take a donkey sight seeing ride in the area and did. Agnes and I chose not to go along. Finally it was time to leave for Addis and we boarded another DC 3 and another scary take off on the muddy dirt runway. Must say despite a few inconveniences and not the best of food and accommodations it was a trip we will never forget.

Ethiopia still has considerable wild animal life, though most of the larger animals such as the elephant, giraffe, and hippo are about extinct. We were able to visit a game park and see some of those left, including wildebeest, zebra, hyena, wart hogs and a variety of antelope. We had heard about this park and decided that we would take our god child to see it.

Living conditions were pretty primitive in the park. We rented two ordinary mobile house trailers that some enterprising Ethiopian had purchased from the US for use in the park. I don't recall how many there were but there must have been a dozen. We had our meals in a makeshift restaurant under a tent. It certainly was not luxurious but it was adequate and we did not mind.

We were able to obtain the services of a guide to show us around in the park and to protect us from any animals that would harm us including humans. And it was indeed fortunate that we had him. On one occasion when we were deep in the woods we were suddenly confronted by a young Danakil tribesman with greasy platted hair armed with a long rifle and knife with a bandolier of ammunition strapped around him.

An armed Danakil tribesman in the Awash River game park, who posed for this picture after we had paid him.

To say the least we were startled, but our guide could speak his language and learned that he would allow us to take his picture for money. We were greatly relieved to learn that this was all he wanted and of course were pleased that he would allow us to take his picture. Should add there was not another person in sight when this incident took place. Don't recall how much we gave him, but not much and I took a picture and was about to take another of John and the Danakil but he wouldn't allow me to until I gave him more money.

It was indeed fortunate that we had a guide. As we learned later some friends visiting this park without guide had suddenly encountered one of these ferocious looking Danakil tribesmen who demanded money of them but offered nothing in return, in other words extorted money from them. They had their young daughter with them and this made them even more afraid. The father proffered a small amount of money and fortunately the Danakil accepted it and did not molest them further. The Danakil are a nomadic tribe that is accustomed to roaming that part of Africa.

Trip to Kenya

After we had lived in Ethiopia for about nine months we decided it was about time to take a short vacation in Kenya, a country that adjoined Ethiopia. Arrangements were made through a tourist agency in Addis. We would travel by air to Nairobi from Addis and by overnight train from there to Mombassa, that is located on the Red Sea. From there we would be met by a taxi and the taken to a beach hotel where we would stay for several days. Believe it or not these plans all worked out well. Of course the train ride was not up to US standards and no ways close to those in England or continental Europe but we made out with minor discomfort.

After a couple of days at the modest resort hotel we decided to rent a car and see some places of interest in the area and later drive the car back to Nairobi, stopping in two of the major game parks in Kenya enroute.

We enjoyed our stay in the hotel though it is not far from the equator and quite hot. We ate and slept in air conditioned facilities and the food was very good.

We met a family from England who were on their way to a new life in Australia. They had sold their farm and all other possessions in England and were planning to buy farm land in Australia and begin anew. The man and wife looked to be in their late thirties and they gave as their reason for the change more opportunity for a better life, especially for their children. We ate with them several times and enjoyed their company.

Part of our days were spent on the beach and once or twice we tried swimming but the water was not very clear and so gave that up. Did enjoy seeing some of the natives who would climb the coconut trees in their bare feet and throw coconuts down for us to open and drink the juice. The beach was not crowded and we enjoyed just sitting and looking out over the Indian Ocean.

Some of our time was spent driving to some of the other resorts located in nearby locations including a premier hotel located on an island that could only be reached by a very crude form of a ferry pulled by hand cranked pulley. After we were on the other side on our way to the hotel we went through a very old deserted village whose remains were in several places wrapped in trees that had grown up around and through them. It gave one a strong feeling of antiquity.

We drove into Mombassa and explored the city. It is Kenya's largest port and is quite old, likely established by the Portuguese in the 1600s. The Muslims are there in large numbers but most of the merchants are Indians. We visited a large mosque there and it was very impressive. We also located a large government warehouse filled with ivory that had been confiscated from poachers. The sale of ivory was prohibited except by government. We looked over the old Fort Jesus (1592). Mombassa is really an interesting old city and full of history.

After about a week in this area it was time to move on and we embarked on a drive back to Nairobi that would take us through two game parks, Tsavo East and West. There were several game park lodges in these parks and we stayed in two of them. During daylight hours, we ventured out in the parks to view the animals in their natural habitats. We were able to see elephants, lions, tiger, giraffe, gazelle, wildebeest, water buffalo, zebra, a variety of antelope, hippo, rhino, and numerous types of birds. These are the ones I can remember but there must have been others.

Two events stand out in my memory. The first was when we were riding slowly through elephant territory and I was in the back seat taking pictures and Agnes was driving. We had a German tourist who was staying at our lodge to go with us that afternoon. Suddenly a mother elephant with her new offspring and her mate loomed up on one side of the road and became frightened and decided to charge us. They had their ears up and were loudly trumpeting. Agnes had stopped the car to let the elephants by but when it appeared they were headed for the car she put the car in reverse and began to back up with her eyes on the charging elephants and backed into the muddy roadside ditch and became stuck. In the meanwhile the elephants still trumpeting loudly veered past us. Visitors to the parks are not supposed to get out of their vehicles while they are viewing the animals but we were forced to in order to get our car unstuck and back on the road. Fortunately, we had the German passenger and the two of us pushing and Agnes driving were able to get the car out and back on the road, one of those unforgettable events that ended well.

The other event was our visit to Mzima Springs that is also located in one of the parks and near one of the lodges we stayed in. The unique feature there is that one can descend to an underwater chamber in the springs and view the hippos, fish, crocodiles and other life swimming underwater in the springs, another unforgettable sight.

After several days in the park we arrived in Nairobi for a bit more seeing of the sights and some shopping before turning in our rental car and boarding a plane for Addis. In Nairobi we stayed in the oldest and most interesting hotel in Nairobi, the Norfolk. It goes back to colonial days and continues many of the customs of those days. Might add we have been to Nairobi a number of times since and always stayed in the Norfolk.

Roxie Comes and We Take a Trip

We invited Roxie, my mother-in-law, to visit us and to our delight and surprise she accepted our invitation. She was 79 years of age at this time but able to travel and enjoyed traveling. She let us know that the pastor of her church who was single and about 35 years of age was coming with her. It seems he had lived for a short while in Ethiopia and when he learned she was going there was delighted to come with Roxie. Roxie purchased the air ticket for him. At that time Roxie headed the vestry in St. Paul's Episcopal Church in Wilmington, which was the pastor's church.

Agnes on an alley leading to a merchant's harem.

The pastor's name was Bob Royal and he was a somewhat flamboyant individual. Before coming to the ministry he was an aspiring actor and had the lead role in a Paul Green play depicting the Lost Colony. He played Manchese the Indian chief. Bob stayed at a downtown hotel and Roxie with us and they were with us for about a week or 10 days. We did all we could to entertain them and I believe they had a memorable time.

Bob being somewhat familiar with Ethiopia and knowing a few people from having been there before was able to entertain himself much of the time. He was able to arrange a meeting with the Head of the Ethiopian Church and had a lengthy audience with him. He was also invited by our Minister to preach in our Church one Sunday.

The most significant event during their stay was a trip by car to Harrar, the hometown of Emperor Haile Selassie. It is located almost due east from Addis, and due to poor roads most of the way, a hard day's drive from Addis. In one place the road ends for several miles and it is necessary to travel down a dry river bed until there is a road. Of course in the rainy season when water is flowing it is not possible to travel by car. I am not sure how one gets to Harrar under such circumstances.

On the occasion of our trip there were two cars. A friend of ours, an American working for GoodYear Tires as its Regional Representative in Ethiopia and several others in that part of the world, was stationed in Addis. We invited him along and he brought with him his wife and his Ethiopian assistant who had traveled that road before to Harrar. He was armed with a sawed off shotgun in the event we encountered robbers. We did not let Bob and Roxie know about the gun. The weather was good and we encountered no problems and arrived in Harrar in late afternoon. Our hotel accommodations were considerably above average and were run by European management. We were most pleased since we would be there three nights. We also found the food to be very satisfactory.

The next three days were spent taking in the sights and doing a bit of shopping. There was a heavy Muslim influence here as evidenced by the number of Muslim owned shops and harems. We visited one jewelry shop that was located in a harem. When you walked in you were almost immediately aware of the eyes of women and children peeping out of holes in the balcony rooms. The merchant was sitting in a chair completely surrounded with overlooking balcony rooms. We were the only customers in the room, and we informed him of what we were looking for and the displays of jewelry began to appear, brought in by a servant. One of the merchant's very young children, a daughter, also appeared and hovered around him sitting is his lap much of the time while we were viewing his wares. All the while we were conscious of eyes staring at us from the balcony rooms surrounding the sales room. I don't recall what we purchased, if anything.

We visited some of the open markets where camels were bringing in merchandise. In Addis and other cities visited in Ethiopia we had not observed camels. Harrar did have a different atmosphere from any other place we had been in the country. The Muslim influence was much in evidence. Soon our time was up and we headed home.

Some of Our Friends in Addis

After our interesting trip it was time to get back into a routine. By now we were well into 1972, and settled in nicely and I was beginning to feel comfortable with my work. We had made several new friends, some American and some Ethiopian. Included in these friends were several from my agency in the Ministry, others from the American Embassy and the couple from GoodYear Tire and Rubber who were with us on the trip to Harrar. Three couples from the International Monetary Fund lived in our apartment complex and we socialized with them often. Also the couple from Good Year lived there, the Brians, and I played golf with Marshall, the husband. I regret that I cannot put names to all these people but all this was about 30 years ago and I never was good at remembering names. I must give Agnes credit for helping me to recall most of the names mentioned here. And oh yes, the Ethiopian Director of the Peace Corps moved into our apartment complex in late 72 or early 73, and we got to know him very well. He was from Wisconsin just outside Madison. Believe we sold him some of our furnishing when we were selling out in preparation for our departure in 1974.

I do recall that one of the Monetary Fund couples was over there to be sure the Addis water supply system worked properly and that the water was safe to drink. Don't believe he or his wife drank the water. I know that Agnes had Tetlech the maid to boil and filter all the water that we drank.

The other two were over there to introduce the Ethiopian Ministry to our American Tax System and help it to develop its own system. I don't believe they were very successful. They managed to get the authorities in Addis to stage unscheduled visits to businesses to collect taxes. Tax values were arbitrarily established on the spot and taxes collected. A major handicap to their tax system was the lack of a proper mail system. There were no home delivery postal addresses because there were no business or home addresses as exists in America or other developed countries. In order to receive mail it was necessary pick it up at the post office. The other two couples were McGinnis and Harmonson. They were concerned with improving the tax system in Ethiopia. I recall that McGinnis's wife became ill and had to be evacuated to the U.S. We kept up with the two couples a number of years after we returned from Ethiopia.

There were two surveyors from Great Britain who also lived in our complex and they were over there to map portions of Ethiopia and to establish a system for surveying property in order record it much as we do in this country. At the time we were in Ethiopia the Emperor owned all land in the country, but changes were in sight.

We also came to know a couple from India, and the husband was over there as an Official Representative of the Indian Government to Ethiopia. I no longer recall just what he did but they lived in the complex and we were with them quite often. Through them met some other Indian officials, who were also quite nice and interesting.

Agnes and Tetlesch shopping at the green grocer Gabriel in Addis.

Mike And Marian

Another couple who became special friends was Mike and Marian Fuchs-Carsch. Mike was over there under a TransCentury Contract as was I, and we both served as advisors to the Ministry Of Agriculture in the same agency. We were both Agricultural Economist. Marian had her Doctorate and at the time was free lancing. She was a linguist speaking at least three languages, English, French and German. I seem to recall that she taught a class of Ethiopians English and perhaps she had other work. She was and is a very talented person. We were together on numerous occasions and became lasting friends. Their marriage did not last but the breakup a few years later was most amicable. Today, some 30 years later Marian is one of our closest friends. More about Marian later. We do not see Mike who has remarried and lives on the West Coast but we still consider him a friend.

Left to Right: Marian Fuchs-Carsch, Agnes and Sandy Ferguson. I took the picture. The ladies went with me to visit one of the projects I was inspecting. I no longer recall the region, but we were out several days.

Don And Sandy

There was another couple over there on a TransCentury contract to advise the Ethiopian University on the Student Registration process, Don and Sandy Ferguson. We saw them on numerous occasions and became good friends. We continue to stay in touch with them by correspondence.

Bob And Martha

After a church gathering at the Church of England, Martha Caldwell (in red plaid) is in center of picture. Our church had a diversity of countries represented in its membership and some of this is evident In the dress of those shown.

Two of our closest friends over there were Bob and Martha Caldwell. Bob was serving as a Regional Labor Attaché for about five countries located in that area of Africa. Ethiopia was included and also served as his Headquarters. One of their three children, Peggy, was with them. Their two sons were older and in college in the States. We met the Caldwells at the Episcopal Church shortly after they arrived in country. In a very short time we became lifelong friends.

While over there we looked to them for guidance in many aspects of overseas living. They were old hands at this while we were on our first overseas assignment. Bob was a hard working dedicated Foreign Affairs Officer and Martha had served overseas for the State Department until she and Bob were married in Egypt during World War II, she was equally dedicated. Together they made a wonderful team and were the most hospitable couple I have ever known. Anyone who has been around a Foreign Embassy has observed the importance of helping those who visit the Embassy to get around in a country they are likely not familiar with. They also like to be entertained and made to feel important.

Bob and Martha were the best host and hostess that I have ever known and there were few visitors to the American Embassy in Addis that did not experience the hospitality of the Caldwells. And they were kind enough to include us among their guest in many of their parties. It was through them that we got to meet such people as Richard Pankhurst the noted English Historian who was living in Ethiopia at that time and who had already written several books on Ethiopia and was to later write more.

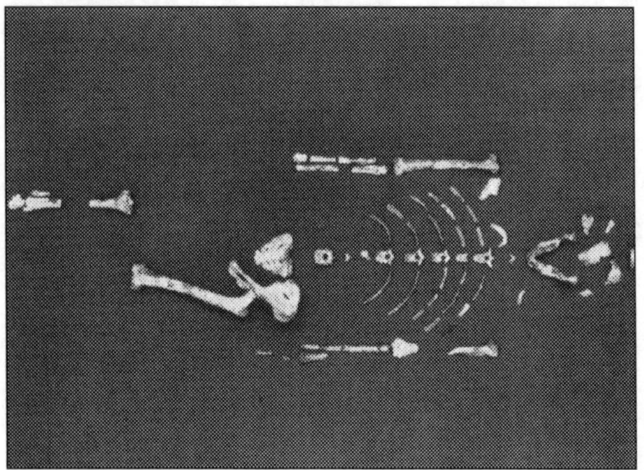

The bones of Lucy that were found by anthropologist while we were in Ethiopia and displayed on the Caldwells' dining room table.

We also met the anthropologist, Don Johansen, leader of the team that discovered the bones of a prehistoric Ethiopian woman whom they called Lucy and later co-authored the book titled Lucy. Actually they made their famous discovery shortly after we left Ethiopia but the Caldwells sent us a picture of the bones of Lucy laid out on their dining room table on Christmas 1974.There were numerous other notable individuals that we met at the Caldwell's home but I no longer recall their names.

By choice the Caldwells lived away from the area where the majority of Official Americans lived, often referred to as the American Ghetto. They had rented an impressive looking home from a well to do Ethiopian family, likely a member of the Royal Family. As mentioned earlier we as well as a number of our other friends had chosen to live outside the ghetto and looking back most of our long time friends from over there also lived outside. A major advantage is we were exposed to the natives and learned more about their customs and way of life. It was just a more broadening experience. We looked down on those who lived in the sheltered ghetto as people who were not very adventuresome.

Flying with Al

Among the numerous activities that I participated in while in Ethiopia were the air flights that I was able to take to several parts of the country. USAID had purchased a new 6 passenger plane that was what is known as a push-pull type with an engine in the front and one in the back. Al, the pilot, had been in Ethiopia for over fifteen years at that time. He began to train Ethiopian Airline pilots when the airline was first being organized, and later to spray locust when Ethiopia was having so much trouble with that insect. After that, he was hired as a pilot For USAID. And did he know more about the geographical layout of that country than anyone I had ever met or heard of! He had flown over most of it and knew where the rivers, lakes, animals, towns and villages were. He had been wounded when he was shot at by smugglers on the ground as he flew along the coast of the Red Sea. He had a favorite story he would tell you about how he had to pick up the body of an American who had been horribly mangled and killed by a crocodile in one of the many swamps and lakes in Ethiopia. The pictures of the body and place where the event took place were hung in a conspicuous place in the cabin and they were gruesome.

It seemed that there was no place of any consequence in that country that Al had not been. I recall one day we were flying and a village loomed up. Al remarked that the village seemed to be completely vacated. He remembered being there last year, and the village being completely occupied. Something had happened since then, maybe a plague of some kind had wiped them out, or maybe they had to leave because of lack of food. And Al wrote down information that would be turned over to proper authorities when we returned to Addis.

There were other trips with Al. One was to Asmara in Eritrea where the United States had a small navy unit stationed to observe activities in the Horn of Africa. Al was well known and liked there, and so I was treated royally. As I recall, we had flown there from the port at Massawa. It is located along the coast of the Indian Ocean not far from the entrance to the Suez Canal. The one thing that sticks in my mind is how miserably hot it was there. The equator is close by and is at sea level. Asmara is only a short distance inland but it is located at a much higher elevation due to the mountains. On our way back to Addis Al flew over the churches at Lalabella. I recall what a thrill it was when he dove close to the church that has a cross on top of it, St. George, the most unique of the group carved out of stone (more about these churches later).

The Social and Political Upheaval Begins

Before we left Ethiopia, the economy and social conditions began to change enough to cause us concern. I must admit that we had not given much consideration to such matters until rather late in my two year contract, but now the "talk" (when the alarming intelligence messages increase) was becoming loud. I am sure some of it was brought about when a drought hit several parts of Ethiopia. The government ignored it until a German magazine brought it to the attention of the world in a rather strident article. Of course I was working in the Ministry of Agriculture that was responsible for action to deal with droughts when necessary, and I had heard something about the situation. Not being any responsibility of mine, I had more or less dismissed the drought, but now that the German magazine had aired the news, I began to pay more attention to the situation. There was a drought, and the Ministry had known about it almost as soon as it began. There was a section in the Ministry whose responsibility was to constantly watch and report crop conditions over the country. There were supplies of food available that could have been sent to the area hit by the drought. Also the Ministry could have sought relief help from foreign countries, but it failed to take action for political reasons. The areas affected were being punished because they were out of favor with the Administration. This assignment in Ethiopia was one of my first major contacts with how government operates in third world countries – and I was learning. Some years later, after working in other such countries, such a situation as the drought in Ethiopia would not have surprised me.

Other events that were taking place in Ethiopia indicated that the drought was only the tip of the iceberg. A rebellious mood in Ethiopia that had been brewing for some time was finally coming out. The country had grown tired of being ruled by a dictator – especially a dictator who thought of himself as a benevolent dictator. In some ways he might have been benevolent, but if he ever had been those days were over. Haile Selassie had grown old, and some thought a bit senile. Times had changed and he had not kept abreast of the changes. He did not recognize or admit that a very limited number of people in Ethiopia controlled the land and other resources in the country, many of them members of his family. More importantly, they were members of the bicameral parliament that was responsible for making the laws governing the country. Of course Haile Selassie held right of veto of any law passed by the parliament, but he was not using this power to favor those needing the help. The foreign governments, especially the United States, who were providing aid and advice to Haile Selassie, were trying to get him to allow the small farmers more freedom to own land. Instead, Haile Selassie was paying more attention to his family than to his foreign advisors. Research in many countries has shown that farmers who own their farms will take better care of them and produce more than those who are farming on land they do not own or control. The feudal system that had existed in Ethiopia for centuries was about to end.

To make matters worse the military was upset with their lack of equipment, pay and conditions in general. There were also numerous other factions in the country who were anxious to rid the country of centuries of rule by dictators. In my opinion, some of this dissatisfaction came to a head after students who had studied abroad, and others who traveled to western countries, returned home. They had observed conditions that came about in developed counties where farmers and others were allowed the freedoms that were missing in Ethiopia. They also observed how people in the western countries were not hesitant to bring pressure on their governments to make changes. Unfortunately, it seems they did not learn enough about the most effective way to bring about these changes. Another factor was the presence of foreigners from the Communistic countries previously mentioned. Plus, the two groups of rebellious military officers (a senior group and junior group) who were likely listening to some of their advice.

After the Christmas holidays were about over, the streets in Addis Ababa became dangerous to travel. In numerous locations crowds would gather to listen to speakers voicing opinions and complaints. The Emperors' soldiers would appear to disperse them in some instances, and arguments would take place. Automobiles – especially those driven by foreigners – were likely to have rocks thrown at them, often badly damaging them.

At times some of these rebellious groups would march down a street and the Emperor's soldiers would take protected positions where they could fire upon them if it became necessary to prevent rioting. I recall almost getting caught up in one of these events. I had just dropped off Agnes at a hair salon where she was to get her hair done. I was waiting for her when I noticed one of these rebellious mobs marching up the street where I intended to park. I quickly realized what was happening, and decided it best not park in such a conspicuous place. The post office was very close by, so I decided I would be less visible to the mob there than on the street where they were marching. I also noticed some of the soldiers were taking positions in the post office area behind the buildings. I thought that maybe I should go back and pick Agnes up before she had her hair done. She could get it done another time when there was no mob in the vicinity, but I realized it too late. The mob was too close and was about to get in between me and the hair salon. There was nothing to do but wait and hope that the salon was not where they were going to stop. Fortunately, it did not take long for the singing and shouting mob to pass.

As soon as they passed and were down the street a good distance, I went back to pick up Agnes. I learned from her that the people in the salon could see the mob marching by and some of them panicked. One of them was so afraid to leave the building after the mob had passed that Agnes volunteered to take her home. We were indeed fortunate not to have gotten mixed up in this event because some of the mob would likely, at the least, thrown some rocks at our car and damaged it. We had already sold our car to Mike and Marian Fuchs-Carsch and they were letting us drive it until we departed Addis in the next few days.

During January and February I took care of any unfinished work I had in the Ministry of Agriculture. I tided up my desk, said a lot of goodbyes and attended a going away party organized by members of my section and others whom I had gotten to know in the Ministry. Agnes and I gave a fairwell party for our closest friends at the Ethiopian Hilton Hotel a day or so before we departed Addis. At one point we were debating whether we should have the party, as the political situation in Addis had reached the point that it was dangerous to be out on the street in a car, but we went ahead and all went well.

At our apartment Agnes and I were planning our trip home. We had first tried to come home by freighter and actually had a reservation. Then about six weeks or so before we were to leave, we were notified that the freighter would not be making the trip and so we had to start all over. We decided that we would complete the trip around the world that had begun when we flew from US to Ethiopia. An excellent travel agent with one of the travel agencies in Addis was able to make the airline and hotel reservations for us.

Our departure from the airport was not easy for us. We were sad and glad – glad to be going home, but sad having to leave Tetalesh. She went to the airport to see us off and likely would have cried but Agnes had said no tears. We had come to like her very much and it was difficult for us to leave her, especially when we knew we would likely never see her again. We were also concerned as to what would happen to her husband who served in the Emperor's body guard. The insurgent group that was in the process of taking over Ethiopia was killing people. Tetalesh had an uncle who was a general that was killed. The Minister of Agriculture, my friend and boss, had been killed. He was married to one of Haile Sellassie's daughters and was a person of influence. Tetalesh's father was a translator for Haile Selassie. Agnes and I do not know what ever happened to Tetalesh. We can only hope for the best.

When we left the Ethiopian airport I was in the cockpit with the pilot. I had been invited there by the chief engineer who was a close friend of one my Indian friends in Addis. He had also upgraded us to first class seats for the flight to India.

The Social and Political Upheaval Begins ◈◈◈◈◈◈◈◈◈◈◈◈

I must say that the view from the cockpit as we took off with a huge roar and all implement lights aglow, was a sight I will never forget. Our first stop was Yemen where we were advised not get off the plane. Agnes was invited to ride in the cockpit when we departed Yemen. Afterwards, we compared notes on our cockpit rides and both concluded there was no way the pilot and the copilot could keep up with all those implement lights that kept tabs on the plane's operations and the flight. But we did appreciate being invited and of course the first class accommodations made the flight much nicer.

We were in India for about a week seeing the sights, including a trip to the Taj Mahal with a car and driver. From India we travelled to Katmandu in Nepal, spending several days there. From there to Bangkok in Thailand, to Hong Kong, and Hawaii. We spent time seeing strange places and people all along the way. Finally, we arrived in San Francisco, then to Washington, DC, and home to Crofton, Maryland. For those who may be interested, a more detailed description of this trip is presented in an earlier book titled, *"Tarboro to Katmandu"*, available through most major book stores.

When we left Ethiopia it was our intention to settle down to a quiet retirement, a bit of travel, a lot of golf, some parties, friends, and whatever came along that appealed to us. We did get several requests to tell our friends about our experiences in Ethiopia and our trip coming home. I had taken slides of much of what we had seen and was able use them to present a pretty good account of what we had experienced. Ethiopia had made a lasting impression on us, and often the thought would cross my mind that I should preserve our experiences in print, maybe a book. Some years later this thought was given a boost when I was asked to hold a class on Ethiopia by the Christopher Wren Association at the College of William and Mary. We were living in Williamsburg, Virginia at the time. I was pleased to receive the invitation, in fact flattered. Fortunately, I had some time to gather information and make an outline of what I would present.

Back to an earlier comment about retirement, our plans for a quiet retirement did not work out. It was not long before the telephone rang, and it was a development agency in Washington. They wanted me to go to another third world country to make a quick assessment of a problem and write a report. I would talk the request over with Agnes and she, with some reluctance, would agree to go with me. This pattern continued for the next sixteen or so years. I finally decided when I was eighty years old that it was time to quit running around to this or that third world country. Now, some thirteen years later and living in Wilmington, NC, my wife's home, I am finally doing my best to write that book on Ethiopia. My apologizes for this brief background note and back to the book *Ethiopia, It's BEGINNING.*

The Beginning of Ethiopia

Ancient Ethiopia

The land that we now know as Ethiopia is millions of years old. What is known about it prior to the beginning of recorded history has been due to the work of anthropologists, paleoanthropologists, and other scientists in what they have been able to conclude from species recovered by various means. As previously mentioned, one of the most important sources of these species has been the Great Rift Valley in eastern Africa. This has been due to past movements in the earth's crust that has exposed deposits of ancient fossils. One of the most celebrated of the species is known as Lucy and was found by a team headed by Donald Johanson in 1974 in the Rift Valley. Lucy lived 3.2 million years ago. She is described as a gracile australopith. The development of humans has been from ape to australopith - a creature that walked upright on two legs (bipedalism), had small canines, or eye teeth (teeth next to the four incisors, or front teeth). This species evolved into homo sapiens (humans) some 100,000 to 40,000 years ago. These humans were distinguished from australopiths by their unique intellectual capacity, and elaborate forms of cultural and communication. They have a throat structure that makes speech possible and their brains are much larger. *Technical data is from *Encarta*.

During the course of researching for this book I came across a review titled *Ethiopia and the Origin of Civilization* and subtitled; *A Critical Review of Ethiopia and the Origin of Civilization*. The subject of this review is presented here on:

A Critical Review of the Evidence of Archaeology, Anthropology, History and Comparative Religion: According to the Most Reliable Sources and Authorities

– By John G. Jackson (1939)

"It is pretty well settled that the city is the Negro's great contribution to civilization, for it was in Africa where the first cities grew up." – F. Haldeman-Julius.

"Those piles of ruins which you see in that narrow valley watered by the Nile, are the remains of opulent cities, the pride of the ancient kingdom of Ethiopia. ... There a people, now forgotten, discovered while others were yet barbarians, the elements of the arts and sciences. A race of men now rejected from society for their sable skin and frizzled hair, founded on the study of the laws of nature, those civil and religious systems which still govern the universe." – Count Volney

"The accident of the predominance of white men in modern times should not give us supercilious ideas about color or persuade us to listen to superficial theories about the innate superiority of the white-skinned man. Four thousand years ago, when civilization was already one or two thousand years old, white men were just a bunch of semi-savages on the outskirts of the civilized world. If there had been anthropologists in Crete, Egypt, and Babylonia, they would have pronounced the white race obviously inferior, and might have discoursed learnedly on the superior germ-plasma or glands of colored folk" – Joseph McCabe

The data in italics is quoted by Jackson in support of his article...

The late Professor George A. Dorsey noted that *"H. G. Wells' heart beats faster in nearly every chapter of his Outline of History, because he cannot forget that he is Nordic, Aryan, English British, white, civilized." (Why We Behave Like Human Beings, p. 40.) This patriotic zeal of Mr. Wells' has, in truth, caused him to suppress certain facts that do not fit into his pet theories"*

In the latest edition of his Outline of History, Mr. Wells ends his chapter on the early empires with the following remarks: *"No less an authority than Sir Flinders Petrie gives countenance to the idea that there was some very early connection between Colchis (the country to the south of the Caucasus) and prehistoric Egypt. Herodotus remarked upon a series of resemblances between the Coichians and the Egyptians."*

(Wells' New and Revised Outline of History, p. 184, Garden City, 1931.) It would have been proper for Wells to have quoted the remarks of Herodotus, so as to give us precise information on the series of resemblances between the Coichians and the Egyptians. Why he did not do so we shall now see. In Book II, Section-104, of his celebrated History, Herodotus states: *"For my part I believe the Coichi to be a colony of Egyptians, because like them they have black skins and frizzled hair."* (See any English translation of The History of Herodotus. The translation by Professor George Rawlinson is the best. See also W.E.B. DuBois, The Negro, p. 31, and Count Volney's Travels in Egypt,of the evidence of Archaeology, Anthropology, History and Comparative Religion: According to the most reliable Sources and Authorities.

The essence of Jackson's review is that Blacks were civilized prior to whites and that the evidence presented in his article here on will prove his claim. I must admit that I was not aware of Jackson's review or the claim made in it, and I expect that there are many others in the same situation. For that reason I decided to mention this article. I will pursue this review long enough to bring it to the attention of those who read this book and to offer a brief comment on the claim made that blacks were the first civilized humans. I have skimmed over the review and note that much of the evidence is based on finding old monuments and statutes showing heads said to resemble those of blacks, thick lips and broad noses, and cultural similarities in different countries. Also many of the claims are rhetorical and assumptive. My question is what happened to the black civilization? And why were the blacks found in Africa in the 1500s and 1600s and on, still living under such uncivilized conditions? In any event the review is interesting and challenging. I do want to clarify one point: the word Ethiopian means a person of a dark complexion (burnt face) and is often used in a generic sense to apply to dark people in general and not just to the country of Ethiopia. The Amhara tribe in Ethiopia never cared to be called Ethiopians because they had the profile of caucasians, sharp noses and thin lips. Also a pure Amhara was much lighter in color than other Africans.

**This document was written by John G. Jackson in 1939 and can be found on the Web. It may be brought up on the computer by typing in the search block of Google the title Ethiopia and the Origin of Civilization.*

Briefly continuing my questioning of Jackson's article: I have reviewed several sections in my Encarta concerning relations between Egypt and Ethiopia in ancient times. I have found several sections that seem to shed more light on Jackson's claim. The earliest civilization arose over 7,000 years ago in Sumer (now Iraq). Sumer grew powerful and prosperous by 5,000 years ago, when it centered on the city-state of Ur. The Mesopotamia region containing Sumer was the same area where people had first domesticated animals and plants. Other early civilizations include the Nile Valley of Northeast Africa, the Indus Valley of South Asia, the Yellow River Valley of East Asia, the Oaxaca and Mexico Valleys, the Yucatan region of Central America, and the Andean region of South America.

All early civilizations had some common features. Some of these included a bureaucratic political body, a military, a body of religious leadership, large urban centers, monumental buildings and other works of architecture, networks of trade, and food surpluses created through extensive farming. Many early civilizations also had systems of writing, numbers and mathematics, and astronomy (with calendars). There were road systems, a formalized body of law, and facilities for education and the punishment of crimes.

As noted here, the land of Sumer is where the earliest civilization took place. The next place mentioned is the Nile Valley of East Africa. Others are also listed, though not necessarily in order. It is in that area where Ethiopia and Egypt, along the Nile Valley, have disputed over land and resources for years. There has been been considerable intermingling of the races. *Another foreign invader appeared, to ride in triumph over the helpless Egyptians. This new power was Ethiopia or Nubia, the state lying to the south of Egypt far up the course of the Nile. Much of the history of Ethiopia is lost. Vague glimpses that we catch of kings and temples there fill us with curiosity.*

They suggest an ancient civilization different from that of Egypt, an art and culture acquired only in part from the Lower Nile. This civilizations was formed partly from Asiatic sources, and partly attained as the native development of an aboriginal negroid race. Thus the ancient kingdom of Ethiopia represents what was probably the highest civilization ever attained by a negro race, or rather by a mingling of negroes and Egyptians. After a while this mixed Ethiopian race seems to have lost its progressive vigor, perhaps under the influx of masses of the wild central African negroes, and sank back into decay. The Ethiopians became once more semi-barbarians, little better than savages.

About eight hundred years before Christ, the Ethiopian armies began invading Egypt. They were not powerful adversaries, but there was no united power to oppose them. Year after year they won their way further down the Nile, re-assimilating the Egyptian culture as they advanced. They became the chief rulers of upper Egypt. At length we find the proud record of their king, Piankhi, stating that the princes of lower Egypt, who were at war among themselves, appealed to him as a protector. He assumed the title of Pharaoh, and marching from end to end of the land reduced it all to obedience (727 B.C.). Even the priesthood thankfully accepted him as the one man who could bring order out of all the turmoil. He was crowned at Thebes with all the ancient ceremonials. A libyan captain had already sat upon the proud throne of the ancient gods; now it was held by an Ethiopian.

More than one of the Pharaohs of this Ethiopian dynasty are mentioned in Bible history. The most important of them after Piankhi was Taharqua, the Biblical Tirhakah. Neither he nor any other ruler succeeded in establishing much authority over the fighting princes, Libyan and Egyptian, who dwelt in the Nile delta, but Tirhakah did gather them all for an incursion into Palestine. There he made alliance with King Hezekiah of Judah and with King Luliya of Tyre, and defeated and plundered the cities which opposed him. He thus brought down upon himself the wrath of the conquering Assyrians, who had seized Syrai and Israel, and who objected to having any one but themselves thus snatch the spoils of Asiatic war.

Of the Assyrian victory of Sennacherib over Tirhakah we already told, and of the subsequent mysterious destruciton of the Assyrian army before Jerusalem. As a result of this struggle came the invasion of Egypt by Esarhaddon, mightiest of the Assyrian monarchs. Tirhakah, unable to oppose him, was now defeated within the borders of Egypt itself, and fled up the Nile to safety in distant Ethiopia. The vassal princes transferred their easy allegiance to Esarhaddon, and he returned to Assyria. Then Tirhakah marched back with a fresh army from Ethiopia, and was again accepted as Pharaoh, in his turn.

Helpless Egypt had become a mere see-saw upon which Assyrian and Ethiopian rose in turn. The next Assyrian sovereign, Assurbanipal, sent his forces once more to the attack. Tirhakah was again defeated and again fled. Says Assurbanipal, "The might of the soldiers of Asshur, my Lord, overwhelmed him and he fled to his place of night." Such of the Egyptians as had been most active in supporting the Ethiopian were carried off to Assyria as prisoners.

Tirhakah died; but his son, Tanutamen, came back in his stead from that dark and mysterious Ethiopia, "the place of night." For a third time, he re-established his country's power over Egypt. Assurbanipal drove him away again. Thus the two foreign powers exhausted each other. * *From Encarta*

This shows how the Nubians and Egyptians spread out to populate countries along the Mediterranean. It does give some credence to Ethiopia having been an early developer of civilization. I still do not agree that these Nubians and Egyptians were of the ethnic stock described by Jackson, nor do I agree that the Greeks learned some of their math from a highly civilized Ethiopian society, as claimed in one article of my *Encarta*.

The country we now call Ethiopia was known as Abyssinia until the 20th century. By the first century A.D. the city of Aksum was the capitol of Ethiopia. It was the leader of a powerful dynasty that traded with such countries as India, China, Persia, and countries along the Mediterranean including Egypt. Ethiopia was fortunate in having a sizeable amount of gold, ivory and slaves. Its gold coins were especially prized. It traded for cotton cloth, glassware, swords, guns, axes, and other manufactured goods.* *Pankhurst*

Feudal System

This country was organized along feudal lines similar to those in the West. At the top was the emperor. Next in line were the lords, followed by the peasants, and at very bottom were slaves. Just as in the West, the emperor ruled by divine right. This was backed by the claim that the first emperor was descended from King Solomon and the Queen of Sheba. It is noted that this system lasted until Haile Selassie was deposed in 1974.

Ethiopia was unique in Africa in that it was the only country having a feudal system so similar to those operating in the western countries. This is likely due to Ethiopia being in close contact with other countries having feudal systems. In addition foreigners working in Ethiopia were another source of information on how other countries were organized. In other countries having feudal systems, the ruler and the lords gradually lost their control over the peasants. Many of the peasants became land owners with deeds to their land. Not so in Ethiopia. When I was in Ethiopia in 1974 the Emperor, Haile Selassie, was for the most part in control of all the land. The idea of individuals having land mapped and deeded to them was just being explored. Undoubtedly, this failure to allow those who tended the land to ever own the land was at least partially to blame for the overthrow of Haile Selassie and those lords who wielded control over them. Haile Selassie and the emperors who preceded him dispensed land as they saw fit, taking the land back when it a suited them. This led to an unstable society. I hasten to add that deeds to land were unknown in most other African countries in those days.

Aksum

Aksum, the first capitol of Ethiopia, was a place to behold in its early days. It was located in Northern Ethiopia about 30 miles or so from the Red Sea. Adulis was its major port and was located on the Red Sea a short distance away. Over the years the various emperors in Aksum had built impressive looking palaces and monuments. The large blocks of stone, some as high as 600 feet and carved out of a single block of stone, were known as stele. These steles had stories of famous battles and other deeds inscribed on them in Sabaean, Ge'ez and Greek. They were then erected into columns. How this was done is not exactly known, but conjecture is they may have been raised up using mounds of dirt and holes dug in the ground to raise them to an upright position.

During the third century A.D., Aksum increased its fame by adding Christianity to its notable history of achievements. It was this event that enabled Ethiopia to lay claim to being the world's oldest Christian empire. How this came about is an interesting story. Prior to introduction of the Christian religion in Ethiopia in 330 A.D. it like many other countries in Africa and elsewhere – worshiped not one god but many. There were gods of love, fertility, war, and others. A statue of Ares, one of the important war gods in Greece, was built by Emperor Ezana. It was his favorite god. If the subject was important it likely had a god represented by a monument, temple, altar or some other object. In Ethiopia the worship of snakes was also common. Evidence of this was found on some of the tablets and monuments in Aksum.

Introduction of Christianity

Prior to the introduction of the Christian religion mention was made that the treasurer of Queen Candace of Ethiopia, a Eunuch, went to Israel to worship the God of Israel. He was baptized and went back to Ethiopia and evangelized some of his people thereby

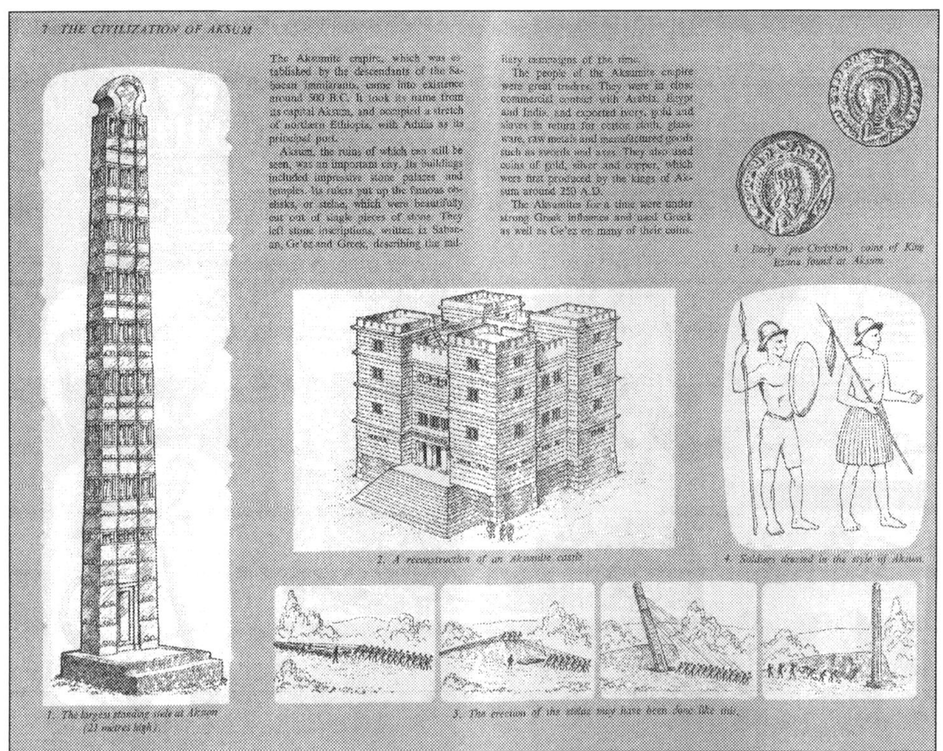

7 THE CIVILIZATION OF AKSUM

The Aksumite empire, which was established by the descendants of the Sabaean immigrants, came into existence around 500 B.C. It took its name from its capital Aksum, and occupied a stretch of northern Ethiopia, with Adulis as its principal port.

Aksum, the ruins of which can still be seen, was an important city. Its buildings included impressive stone palaces and temples. Its rulers put up the famous obelisks, or stelae, which were beautifully cut out of single pieces of stone. They left stone inscriptions, written in Sabaean, Ge'ez and Greek, describing the military campaigns of the time.

The people of the Aksumite empire were great traders. They were in close commercial contact with Arabia, Egypt and India, and exported ivory, gold and slaves in return for cotton cloth, glassware, raw metals and manufactured goods such as swords and axes. They also used coins of gold, silver and copper, which were first produced by the kings of Aksum around 250 A.D.

The Aksumites for a time were under strong Greek influence and used Greek as well as Ge'ez on many of their coins.

1. The largest standing stele at Aksum (33 metres high).

2. A reconstruction of an Aksumite castle.

3. The erection of the stelae may have been done like this.

4. Soldiers dressed in the style of Aksum.

5. Early (pre-Christian) coins of King Ezana found at Aksum.

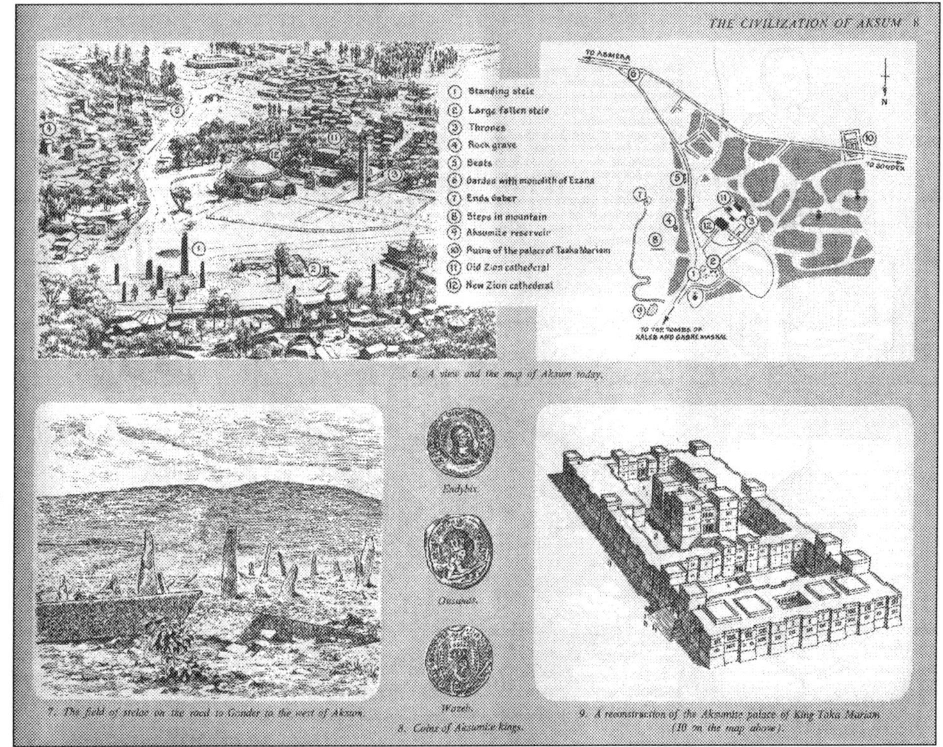

THE CIVILIZATION OF AKSUM 8

6. A view and the map of Aksum today.

7. The field of stelae on the road to Gonder to the west of Aksum.

Endybis.

Ousanas.

Wazeb.

8. Coins of Aksumite kings.

9. A reconstruction of the Aksumite palace of King Taka Mariam (10 on the map above).

*Information from **A history of Ethiopia in Pictures** by Geoffrey Last & Richard Pankhurst –Illustrated by Eric Robson.*

introducing Christianity to Ethiopia. It should be noted that some of the foreigners in that country were Christians. However, the major introduction of Christianity in Ethiopia came about in 330 A.D. when the Emperor of Ethiopia, Ezana, became a Christian. *From: The Church of Ethiopia.*

How this happened is one of the interesting legends of Ethiopia. It seems that a philosopher, Meropius from Tyre (then the most important city of Phoenicia, located at present day site of Sur in southern Lebanon), set out to visit India. He was accompanied by his two nephews Frumentius, and Aedesius. They stopped in a port along the coast of Africa when they ran short of food. It turned out that the inhabitants were hostile to Roman citizens at that time, and all were murdered except the two young nephews. They were taken to the Emperor of Aksum and soon gained his interest and confidence. Aedesius was made his cup bearer, and Frumentius – the elder – who showed signs of wisdom and maturity, and was made his treasurer. It was not long before the king became ill and died. His wife was left with an infant son as heir to the throne. She begged Frumentius and Aedesius to stay even though the dying king had given them permission to return home. She wanted them to help her administer the kingdom until her son grew up. They acceded to her wish and remained to serve her well. *From: The Church of Ethiopia.*

As time passed, Frumentius began to think about the religion of the country. There was little knowledge of Christianity, but there were some foreigners who were Christian. Frumentius met with them and encouraged them to spread the Word of God and to establish meeting places. For this he accorded them favors and helped them in any way he could. This enabled him to gradually spread the Word. Eventually the young King Ezana became a convert. When Ezana became old enough to rule, Frumentius and Aedesius asked permission to leave the country. Aedesius returned to his home in Tyre, but Frumentius went to Alexandria, Egypt and begged the new Patriarch, Athanasius, to appoint a bishop to administer to the growing number of Christians in Aksum. The Patriarch appointed a committee to consider the request and it concentrated Frumentius first Bishop of Aksum.

The information in last four paragraphs is from a book titled ***The Church of Ethiopia*** *published by the orthodox church of Ethiopia and authored by a committee made up of distinguished scholars. It was published in connection with the meeting of the Central Committee of World Council of Churches in Addis Ababa in 1971. It is a brief history of the Church of Ethiopia.*

King Ezana was serious about religion and began to encourage his lords to become Christians and they in turn prevailed upon their vassals to join. As an inducement the King granted land to his lords to be used for a variety of church purposes. In this manner Christianity spread from the top down, rather than from the bottom up as was the case in most other countries.

From Solomonic to Falashan Rule

King Lalibela and His Famous Rock Churches

There were eleven of these churches carved out of solid volcanic rock in the vicinity of Roha, the capital of King Lalibela in Lasta. The name of the capital Roha was later changed to Lalibela in honor of the king. Other churches had been carved from solid rock, but none as wonderful as these, nor for reasons so unique. It seems that Lalibela had been exiled to Jerusalem by his half brother King Harbay and was living there when Jerusalem was taken over by Saladin, the famous Muslim conqueror. When he returned to Ethiopia after a twenty five year exile and regained the throne, he wanted Roha to become the New Jerusalem.

To this end he named the river running through Roha the Jordan, and one of the eleven churches, Beta Gotha, was designed to symbolize the Church of Holy Sepulchre in Jerusalem. A hill in the Roha area was called Debra Zeit (Mount of Olives) to represent the place where Christ was captured. There is considerable interest and some controversy as to who actually designed the churches. Doresse believes that the work has been attributed to workmen from Jerusalem or Egypt. Hancock, author of *The Sign and Seal*, thinks the Knights Templar may have been the "true artificers of the Lalibela churches." It is true that while Lalibela was in exile in Jerusalem, he knew and had ample opportunity to associate with the Templars. Furthermore, in one of the churches Hancock noticed crosses that he believed to be Crusader crosses. Also it was known that the Templars had been associated with the construction of magnificent churches in other countries.

Hancock had this to say about the construction of the churches: "the churches remain places of living worship eight hundred years after they were built. It is important to stress however, that they were not built in the conventional sense, but instead were excavated and hewn directly out of the solid red volcanic tuff on which they stand. In consequence, they seem superhuman – not only in scale, but also in workmanship and in conception." The churches are connected by a complex labyrinth of tunnels and narrow passageways offset crypts, grottoes, and galleries. Hancock thinks the most striking of them is the Beta Giorhis (the Church of Saint George). I have also seen these churches and I agree with his choice. Hancock believes "the eleven churches of Lalibela were the most architecturally advanced buildings that Ethiopia had ever known…and in opinion of UNESCO, they deserved to be ranked amongst the wonders of the world." Hancock was interested in the churches because of the possibility that some clues might be obtained from the churches that would help him locate the Ark of the Covenant, the object of his search. Various speculations as to who might have built the churches have been made, but Hancock says no one seems to know who actually built them or exactly how. There were even some who said the angels had built them. This is just another of the mysteries that make Ethiopia a strange place indeed.

Falashans

Another strange event associated with the history of this period in Ethiopia is how the Solomonic succession to the throne had been interrupted. A coup d'état led by a chieftainess by name of Gudit had overthrown the Solomonic emperor in Axum. This Gudit adhered to the Jewish faith and was head of a large tribal confederation of Agaw. It was from this tribal group that the Falashans, or black Jews, came. Some fifty years after Gudit died, the Zagwe monarchs, who came out of the Agaws, had succeeded in uniting most of northern Ethiopia. It is noted that when Gudit killed the Solomonic emperor in Axum, two of the emperors sons were also killed. One escaped, thus assuring the Solomonic line was preserved. That line was begun by King Solomon and the Queen of Sheba. The Zagwe claimed to be descended from some of the Jewish servants who had accompanied young Menelik I when he had returned to Ethiopia from Jerusalem. The new dynasty of Gudit was based on a legendary marriage with the daughter of one of the last rulers of Axum. According to Doresse, this royal line was of ancient Agaw blood.

Doresse notes there are several stories as to how the Solomonic line to the throne of Ethiopia was restored. One version had the last Zagwe ruler being murdered and the Solomonic line being restored. This version however, was superseded by another that had an influential Monk, Takla-Haymanot, interceding to influence the Zagwe ruler to abdicate in favor of Yekuno-Amlak. The latter version appears to be the more likely one. The Zagwe rule had lasted for some three hundred years, and finally ended rather peacefully. Ethiopia experienced a period of rapid development that was to continue for some two hundred years. Dorsee reports that "territorial unity was once more established, civil and religious institutions were rigorously codified, and literature and art began to flourish again." As usual, the Muslims were threatening to overthrow the kingdom of Ethiopia.

With a Return to Solomonic Rule

Prester John

No story about the history of Ethiopia is complete without discussing the fabled story of "Prester John". I came across a reference to him in Jean Doresse's book titled "Ethiopia", in the Introduction section. There it notes that about 1165 A.D. Western Europe first began to take an interest in a mysterious ruler by the name of Prester John. This was about the time Muslims were a force to be reckoned with in the Mid East, especially in the Holy Land and the eastern shores of Africa, including Ethiopia. It was after the death of Emperor Na'od when Queen Helena was ruling as regent for her son Lebna-Dengel that interest in Prester John increased. Queen Helena consulted with Pedro de Covilham, a Portuguese living in Ethiopia. She decided upon his advice to send Mathew the Armenian to the court of the Portuguese to ask for help in combating the Muslims who were taking over the Ethiopian ports along it's coast. She served as the ruler until her son became of age some years later (his rule discussed heron). The letter was signed Prester John and was sent to Emanuel, Prince of Constantinople, and so the first letter to reach a Western nation was likely written by Queen Helena, widow of Emperor Na'od.

My curiosity was roused, and I decided to use Prester John as a keyword on the Encarta. Up comes John Buchan, first Baron of Tweedsmuier, as the author of a book titled *Prester John*, published in 1910. It seems the Baron was a politician who also liked to write. He was the British ambassador to Canada at one time. His book, a novel, was published in 1910. It was picked up by the noted film producer Lord Alfred Hitchcock and made into a motion picture in 1935. I was able to read most of the book, and to my disappointment, learned the setting for this book and film was in South Africa rather than in Ethiopia where the story of Prester John really began. I enjoyed the book. It was a real thriller about how the rebellion of a tribe in South Africa was thwarted by a young British chap. He was in South Africa when he accidently discovered a valuable necklace of rubies and other precious stones belonging to the mysterious Prester John while he was employed in an outpost trading store.

While engaged in looking for additional information on Prester John, I came across a book by Elaine Sanceau titled *The Land of Prester John: A Chronicle of Portuguese Exploration*. It was published in 1944 and I was able to get a copy and find it provides much valuable information on Ethiopia and the mythical Prester John. Now back to letter to Emanuel of Constantinople. I should mention it is five pages and abridged. I shall shorten it further. Also I note the letter is written *for* Prester John and not *by* him. The letter begins as follows: *"John, priest by the almighty power of God and the might of our Lord Jesus Christ, King of Kings and Lord of Lords, to his friend Emanuel prince of Constantinople , greetings , wishing him health , prosperity and continuance of divine favor. Our majesty has been informed that you hold our Excellency in love and that the report of our greatness has reached you. Moreover, we have heard through our treasurer that you have pleased to send us some objects of art and interest that our Exaltedness might be gratified...the Lord of Lords: "surpasses all others under heaven in virtue, riches, and in power; seventy-two kings pay us tribute. In the three Indies our Magnificence rules, and our land extends beyond India. It reaches towards the sunrise over the wastes, and it trends toward... Babylon near the Tower of Babel. Seventy two provinces, only a few of them Christian, serve us. Each has its own king, but all are tributary to us".* –Pg.1-ltr.

The letter continues describing the great variety of wild animals, elephants, tigers, white bear, wild oxen, red lions, wild horses, and more. Wild men, cyclops and similar women are cited. Men with horns, and one-eyed men are mentioned as are men with eyes in front and back of their heads. Men who eat the flesh of men and who never fear death are cited. The writer continues to talk of the greatness of the lands of Prester John, its minerals, precious stones, and everlasting youth for those who partake of the waters of a spring that flows at foot of Mount Olympus. This spring is said to be only three days journey from the paradise out of which Adam was driven. A fountain is mentioned that purges Christians and would be Christians from all transgressions (there seems no end to all the wonderful miracles in the land of Prester John).

There are even worms called salamanders that can only live in fire. They build cocoons like silkworms that are unwound by the ladies of the palace and spun into cloth and dresses. In order for the dresses to be cleaned, they must be cast into flames.

"When we go to war, we have fourteen golden and bejeweled crosses borne before us instead of banners. Each of these crosses is followed by ten thousand horsemen and one hundred thousand foot soldiers, fully armed, without reckoning those in charge of the luggage and provision." – Pg.3-ltr.

"All riches, such as are upon the world, our Magnificence possesses in superabundance."– Pg.4-ltr.

Kings wait upon Prester John, performing the duties of body servants. Perhaps the most amazing claim is the following: *"Before our palace stands a mirror, the ascent to which consists of five and twenty steps of porphyry and serpentine...This mirror is guarded day and night by three thousand men. We look therein and behold all that is taken place in every province and region subject to our scepter."* – Pg4-ltr.

With a Return to Solomonic Rule

This remarkable letter and others similar to it circulated around European countries for over two centuries. This corresponded with the crusades in the Holy Land and the battles taking place in Ethiopia, particularly those along the Red Sea and the Indian Ocean. The struggle between Ethiopia and the Muslims had been going on since about 800AD. Ethiopia had lost control of its coastal ports, and its capital at Aksum was a relic of what it had been. Most of its trade with the outside world had ceased. The ruling monarch had deserted Aksum in favor of a moving capitol.

According to Jean Doresse, 1200 A.D. was about the time when Western Europe was beginning to find out something of Ethiopia. He notes that it was around 1165 A.D. when rumors began to spread around Europe that an immensely rich Emperor similar to the one described in the previously mentioned 1165 letter existed in Ethiopia. This was good news for those European countries engaged in fighting the Muslims. and also for the Ethiopians who had lost its ports to the Muslims and were in danger of losing some of its interior possessions. Both Doresse and Sanceau stated Portugal was the first European country to conclude Ethiopia was where Prester John was located. They sent an embassy that actually reached Ethiopia and made contact with Lebna-Dengel David II (his mother, Queen Helena supposedly had sent a Prester John letter to the King of Portugal). Other countries tried to send embassies to Ethiopia but for one reason or another they failed to reach it.

Many years earlier Pedro da Covilham, a Portuguese had come to Ethiopia and the Ethiopian ruler would not permit him to leave. This seemed to be a common practice to not allow foreigners to leave once they came to Ethiopia, especially if they could contribute to the development of the country. Pedro was educated and above average. He was well treated by the Ethiopians and decided to make himself content with living there. If asked, he would serve as an advisor to the ruler of Ethiopia. One such occasion was during the time Queen Helena, widow of Emperor Na'od was ruling as regent until her son Lebna-Dengel became of age to take over as Emperor. Pedro was asked about the advisability of sending a messenger to Dom Manuel, King of Portugal, with a message asking for military assistance. He specifically wanted a fleet to seize the Ethiopian ports from the Muslims who had taken them over. Pedro thought the idea had merit and suggested sending Mathew the Armenian. Unfortunately, due to unforeseen events it took Mathew four years to reach Portugal with the message. The Portuguese responded by sending an Embassy headed by Dom Rodrigo. In the intervening years, as we will see the young Emperor, Lebna-Dengel had taken over from his mother Queen Helena and conditions in that country had undergone some unexpected changes.

The Portuguese Embassy Arrives

The book written by Elaine Sanceau contains a very elaborate description of the reception the Portuguese Embassy received from the new Emperor, Prester John (as the Portuguese insisted on calling him). To set the stage, I shall introduce the main characters. The embassy was sent by Dom Manuel, king of Portugal. The leader of the Embassy was Dom Rodrigo, a seasoned diplomat. Mathew the Armenian came along to serve as interpreter but became ill and died soon after the embassy arrived. Also in the embassy party was the legendary Padre Francisco Alvares who later travelled extensively in Ethiopia and wrote a very popular book of his travels. His book is quoted by all the latter historians such as Doresse, Pankhurst, and others. Pedro da Covilham, who was already living in Ethiopia, was picked up by his countrymen as an advisor, particularly as to the customs of the Ethiopians.

On the Ethiopian side there was Lebna Dingel Dawit, or as the Portuguese insisted on calling him, Prester John, or at times David, a young king of twenty. David had begun his military career at the young age of seventeen when he met the enemy of his country, Emir Mahfuzh, on the plains near Zeila and defeated him. It was a great victory and the young Emperor was held in high esteem by his subjects. He was no longer under the tutelage of Queen Helena who had brought him up well. He proved to be a very competent ruler, and was now in complete charge. The queen had no desire to rule after her son became of age, and as mentioned he had absorbed her tutelage well.

They were greeted by one of the emperor's staff and were provided with a spacious gay colored tent intended for royalty. The emperor and his staff, including military, were no longer headquartered in Aksum. The capital was now located about the country as dictated by the emperor. The emperor would select an area of the country that suited his purposes, and notify the lord whose land was to be occupied that he was setting up the capital there. It must have been somewhat like a big circus or carnival moving in and setting up all the tents. Then there were the camp followers. They were mostly women who ranged from the ladies of the emperor's court to the courtesans – or as Pankhurst describes them – the equivalent of Japanese geisha girls. Nearly every soldier had at least one wife. These camp followers were assigned duties such as preparing the enjara (Ethiopian dish, a large pancake made of flour from teff, a grain, and containing a variety foods such as beans, rice, chicken, lamb, goat, other meats, and vegetables), tej (fermented honey, a strong drink), for the nobility, and talla (homebrew) for the soldiers.

The Portuguese Embassy Arrives

As mentioned, the young emperor had only recently won a sizeable victory over the Muslims and he was pleased with himself. He was not so much in need of the Portuguese as when the message from his mother, the queen, had been sent some four years earlier. This likely accounted for his less than cordial treatment of the embassy with respect to an initial meeting with Dom Rodrigo and his staff.

The story as reported by SANCEAU is that a message was sent to Rodrigo that the embassy was free to sell their wares and to purchase goods from the Ethiopians. This appeared harmless, but it failed to take into account that Rodrigo considered this an insult. It was beneath him and his staff to engage in such grossly plebian activities. The embassy was there to engage in much more important matters. The emperor purposefully delayed the first meeting to show his displeasure with Dom Rodrigo's reply to the offer to allow the Portuguese to trade in Ethiopia. Also he was not satisfied with the gifts offered by the Portuguese. Dom Manuel had selected some elegant furniture and other items as gifts and word had reached the Ethiopian Emperor of this. These rich items had never reached Ethiopia and Dom Rodrigo was forced to come up with whatever he could scrape together as gifts. Among the items were four bales of pepper, highly valued in those days in Europe and Ethiopia. The pepper was not originally planned as a gift, but Rodrigo realizing the original gifts were not sufficient, had added the pepper. The gifts including the pepper were pompously paraded into the emperor, but he was not pleased. To show his displeasure he did not meet with Dom Rodrigo that day. Instead, he asked that the embassy turn over all the pepper they had. Pepper was used as money at that time. Rodrigo was reluctant to get rid of all the pepper but did give up most of what the embassy had. In addition some fancy travelling trunks were given, but Prester John was still not satisfied. The next request was for a pair of breeches. Two pair were turned over, but still Prester John was not ready to hold a meeting.

At this point the Portuguese began to worry that they would never be allowed a meeting, and worse they would not be permitted to leave the country. This fear was based on the fact that there were many foreigners in Ethiopia who had not been permitted to leave. Members of the embassy had talked with them and learned they had become resigned to their fate and decided to make the best of life in Ethiopia. Some had intermarried with Ethiopians or with foreigners from different countries. All had learned Amharic, the most common Ethiopian language. To make the waiting even more intense, rumors were spread that the Portuguese would be held indefinitely. Invitations to meet were issued and before they could take place they were cancelled. It did look bleak to the embassy.

Another time a meeting was called during the night. This time the meeting was actually held. It was not face to face with Prester John (Lebna-Dengel), but with a curtain between Prester John and members of the embassy. Messengers ran back and forth between the two parties with questions and answers. First, Prester John wanted to know where all the lavish presents were that had been promised by the Portuguese ruler when Mathew the Armenian met with him. This information, as previously mentioned, had reached Prester John. Dom Rodrigo explained that the shipment would come with the next embassy, a higher level embassy that was to follow the present embassy. This did not satisfy Prester John as he was suspicious that Dom Rodrigo was not telling him the truth, and so he continued to postpone a face to face meeting.

There were more curtain meetings on a variety of subjects. The young Ethiopian ruler had an insatiable desire to know everything about the Portuguese. He wanted to know about their religion and how it compared with Ethiopia. Father Alvares handled the religious questions from the young ruler and they were thoughtful and penetrating. His mother the queen had taught him well. He put Father Alvares to the test. There were questions about the Portuguese king, how many wives did he have? How many children did he and his wife have? How they took their meals, and where they lived? He wanted to know about the Portuguese arms, fortifications, the size of the country and about its foreign possessions. He had the Portuguese fire their small arms. Also he had them use their swords in a mock duel. And he even had them dance and sing for him. This would seem insulting, but the Portuguese never hesitated and performed well.

The young emperor wanted to know about the differences between the Latin church and the Ethiopian Coptic Church. For example did the members of the Latin church always obey the Pope? To which Francisco Alvares replied "most always". What about a matter that was not religious and Francisco replied yes? The young emperor said should that happen in his country, "the Ethiopians would throw the edict in the fire!" Francisco then explained this could never occur in the Latin church. The Pope being the Holy Father, "his mandates could never be in opposition to the Holy Writ." On the contrary "it was the Scriptures that inspired them all". Then he went on to explain that the Pope was guided by a host of knowledgeable people such as doctors, cardinals, archbishops, and bishops. "Such learned persons," he added, "were sadly lacking in Ethiopia!"

Sanceau noted that the question of the Trinity never came up and this was fortunate because this is the basic difference between the Latin and Coptic beliefs. The religious discussions went well and helped to cement relations between the two countries – both found good things say about the other's religion. Dom Rodrigo and his group finally were allowed to meet with the emperor face to face, with no curtain. It was explained that the emperor only met with his subjects in the open three times during the year, Christmas, Easter, and Pentecost. There were a few exceptions, his favorites.

The occasion of their first meeting without the curtain was at night, and a cold one. To make it even worse they had to wait at the door for three hours. When they were finally admitted it was a sight to behold. The emperor was sitting on a platform six steps high with a tall crown of gold and silver on his head, richly adorned. He had a silver cross in his hand, and a blue taffeta veil covered the lower part of his face. This was moved aside now and then. He wore a large brocaded robe over a silk shirt, and had a lap robe of gold over his knees. The emperor was young, not very black in complexion, of medium height, and good looking.

After compliments were exchanged the business began. Prester John said he would be pleased if the Portuguese would build forts at Masssawa and Suakin and he would provide provisions. He also invited the Portuguese to capture Zeila. Dom Rodrigo said the capture should be easy as the Moors fled when the Portuguese king sent his fleet in force.

The sequel to the Prester John story is that after Rodrigo had made the agreement with the Ethiopian emperor, a letter in Amharic to the Portuguese king had to be written before the embassy could depart to Massawa to catch the Portuguese fleet back to Portugal. The fleet was due between February and April of 1521and would leave no later than end of April or risk having to stay in port for three months until after the monsoon had come and gone. It seems the emperor was in no hurry to write the letter and the embassy spent Christmas as the guest of the emperor. To shorten the story, it was five years later before the embassy arrived in Portugal. Sanceau was able to provide most of the details of the embassy's sojourn over that period, but that would have been a bit much to present for purpose of this book. Sanceau is a good writer and presents much factual detail in an interesting manner.

A Muslim, Ahmed the Gran, Terrorizes Most of Ethiopia

In 1526 the request and proposals of the Ethiopians were put before the Portuguese and it was not long before the mystery of Prester John was known to Western Europe. Back in Ethiopia conditions were not as good as when the young emperor Lebna-Dengel had defeated the Muslims on the plains near Zeila. A new Muslim figure had come upon the scene, Ahmed-al Ghazi, whom the Ethiopians called Gran (Gran in Amharic means left or left handed). His followers, the Adal Muslims in the tribes of Somalia, and the Dankil, also in the coastal city of Hagar looked upon him as the INMAN OF THE FAITHFUL. He came into power when the Sultan of that region offended his subjects and they rebelled. The Gran slew the Sultan. He was looked upon as a saint by the Muslims and over the next fifteen years from 1527 to 1542 he fought a Holy war with the Ethiopians.

Doresse has summarized the period when the Gran terrorized the high plateaus of major parts of Ethiopia, places such as Dawaro, Amhara, Shoa, and Lasta. Churches, monasteries and the beautiful and priceless treasures that belonged to church and state were taken and the buildings destroyed. People were killed. Some of the most revered of the church property such as the Debra-Libanos, and the church of the Holy Trinity were looted and pillaged. Doresse describes the interior of the Holy Trinity, "The whole of the interior, up to the ceiling, shone with gold and silver plaques inlaid with pearls and decorated with figures of various kinds." He says the whole place was burned to the ground and there is no reliable description of the exterior of church left. Many other Christian sanctuaries containing fabulous precious items that were looted by the Gran are described. But finally it had to come to an end.

The Portuguese Return

The Portuguese to the Rescue Again

Throughout most of this period Lebna-Dengel, the emperor who had been so high handed with the Portuguese embassy headed by Rodrigo, had been in battle after battle with the Gran and was beaten each time. He had sent a message to the Portuguese asking for help, and finally in 1541 the Portuguese sent 400 troops under command of Don Christofe de Gama. By this time Lebna-Dengel had died and his son Claudius (1540-1559) had taken over as emperor. The Portuguese, undoubtedly, were still pursuing the idea of converting the Ethiopians to Catholicism and to more control of the country in general. Earlier Lebna-Dengel had made an agreement with the Portuguese somewhat to this effect, especially as it related to strengthening the Ethiopian military. Of course the Portuguese likely were probably looking beyond the military aspects. In any event the 400 volunteers had arrived. As soon as the rainy season ended they were ready to go after the Muslims. The Gran had been continuously victorious over nearly fifteen years, conquering and looting most of Ethiopia in the process. The troops brought with them some eight cannons, a hundred muskets and an ample supply of side-arms. The first battle was with the Tigrean troops who were between the Portuguese and King Claudius who was in Shoa. The territory was high plateau country that necessitated steep climbs with arms, ammunition and artillery being back packed, sometimes for as much as three days at a time. At the same time, the 400 volunteers were being blocked by the Muslims. In spite of these obstacles the Muslims were defeated, but there was more fighting to be done in this high country.

After a pause for the rainy season in the vicinity of Makalle, the Gran reorganized his army and increased its fighting ability. They added some 900 musketeers and ten cannon provided to him by the head of the Turks in Arabia. The Gran did not wait for the end of the rainy season but began his push through the mud. This time he defeated Don Christofe, captured and tortured him before putting him to death. Fortunately, Claudius was able to combine with his forces the remaining 200 Portuguese. In the next battle of this conflict the Gran, believing he was safe from the Ethiopians dismissed his Turkish allies and was soundly defeated. The Gran was killed by a musket ball and his troops were decimated. The war that had lasted for fifteen years and almost destroyed Ethiopia was over. Doresse notes that: *"The Muslim occupation had brought about ruin on the country, not only in a material sense, but also morally, which was worse."* He goes on to point out that many subjects who had been loyal to Ethiopia had shifted over to the Muslims over the fifteen year period. They were not likely to return, even in spite of a special effort by the church, a ceremonial rite of reconciliation.

Romance

These struggles were not devoid of romance, and battles were often at least partially fought over a beautiful woman. Don Christofe took the wife of and Emir who was a great beauty after the battle he won. In another instance, a Muslim leader Nuir-ibn-al Wazir who undertook a battle to avenge the death of the Gran, did so partially to win the favor of the Gran's widow, another beauty, whom he desired. Incidentally, it was this leader who built the wall around Harare that still stands. In the battle that took place, the Muslim leader was faced by King Claudius, the Ethiopian leader who it was said: would have been less eager to enter the fray had it not been for the love of a woman who, according to the Chronicle, tried to restrain him from doing so. Claudius had taken her from her previous husband who was a priest. Racked with remorse for what he had done, he flung himself in to the thick of the battle and was promptly killed and beheaded.*
**Information on this section provided by Sanceau and Doresse*

Sarsa-Dengel (Molak-Sagad)

Following the rule of King Claudius, the next ruler of significance is Sarsa-Dengel (1563-1597). He had a number of political adversaries including the nobles who generally fought among themselves to determine who would be the next king. Sarsa eliminated them and was eventually crowned at Aksum with the throne name of Malak-Sagad (in english, 'The Kings Adored Him'). He proved to be a good emperor and engaged in successful campaigns against the Galla and Falashans. He also fought battles in the Sudan that were especially appreciated by his countrymen. They even secured control of the prosperous kingdom of Enarya by instituting Christianity there. He forced the Turkish Pasha to negotiate a settlement over the port of Arkiko. According to Doresse, his most important achievements lay in his expeditions against the heathen Gambo tribes and the Galla, and extended the kingdom once more as far as Jaffa. He conquered the Agaw-meder, and paved the way for the eventual pacification of the Semen. He died in 1597 and the country was again in a turmoil deciding who would rule in his place.

An aside, I don't believe we in America fully appreciate one of the major benefits we have – that of democratic elections to determine who will be the president when it is time to elect a new one. Certainly, Ethiopia never enjoyed this privilege for over two thousand years. And it finally took a bloody coup in 1974 followed by seventeen years of Communistic rule to put in place a new ruler by peaceful means.

Emperor Susenyos-1608

After Malak-Sagad's death, a prolonged struggle for a successor was underway. Susenyos, one of the royal princes, finally emerged as the ruler. Without going into all the details, and qualifications, the struggle to become the ruler, as contained in Doresse's History, is presented. He was a royal prince who had fallen into the hands of the Galla at an early age. This had enabled him to escape the customary confinement in the fortified monastery at Geshena accorded most royal princes. A Galla chief had raised him as a son until he was rescued, and this was to prove helpful to him later. Susenyos was with Emperor Sarsa-Dengel on his last expedition, the one that failed, and Susenyos used his wits to escape by taking refuge with some monks. He used his friendly relationship with the Galla to raise armies and successfully attacked some of his enemies. At one point he was defeated and sent into exile.

His time had not arrived. Za-Dengel, a formidable opponent, was chosen to be king, but he had leanings to Catholicism and was excommunicated by the ABUNA. This was done despite the loyal support of his troops who were descended from the Portuguese.

Susenyos had by now acquired some additional support from the nobles and was offered the crown in December of 1604. He accepted, but before the crown could be placed upon his head, another contender named Jacob had to be dealt with before he could have the crown. Jacob was backed by another group of nobles who wanted to place him upon the throne and called upon Susenyos to withdraw. History says his reply was dignified and to the point. *"Even if our late Emperor Malak-Sagad, who was greater than all the rest, were to return from the dead this day, I would not take from my head the crown that has been placed upon it."* (It is not clear when the crown was actually put upon his head, but it seems to have taken place after Susenyos defeated Jacob in battle). The usual method of settling the dispute was undertaken. Jacob's powerful ally Za-Selassie was defeated in battle and then Jacob was soundly defeated. After this in 1608, Susenyos was crowned with all honors at Aksum.

Susenyos proved to be an outstanding ruler and was able to keep the Galla in check and assimilate many of them. He fought against the Agaw and put down a revolt by the Gideon king of the Falasha. He made war on the Muslim state of Fung. The most serious of all Susenyos problems were however, religious. Going back to the reign of Lebna-Dengel there had been an understanding that at some point Catholicism would replace the Coptic form of religion. From time to time this question had arisen, particularly by the few remaining Portuguese and their offspring in Ethiopia. One such case was that of Za-Dengel's conversion to Catholicism that caused so much opposition that he was overthrown. There was much argument, pro and con, for a change to Catholicism. The Latins were skillful in putting across their arguments in ways that people could understand. Even the Coptic bishops admired the Latins in the way they went about converting the Coptics to Catholicism. In addition, the Coptic bishops had become lax and some had committed rape and adultery. Many of the nobles also admired the skill of the Latins. In view of this show of acceptance, Susenyos decided to have the country revert to Catholicism. This brought up the problem of sending a communication of his decision to Rome. Without going into the details, the message was long delayed by a number of difficulties. This allowed time for those who opposed the change to better organize against the action, and there were many who opposed. Susenyos wasted no time in putting his decision into effect even though his message to Rome had not been delivered. He banned the observance of the Sabbath and went to a Latin priest for confession. He publicly announced his conversion to Catholicism in Aksum.

In spite of all the fanfare to convert to Catholicism, Ethiopia revolted against the idea. Doresse and others observe that the conversion should have been planned on a more gradual basis. The measures taken to bring it about were uncompromising and unacceptable. For example, all Christian Ethiopians had to be re-baptized and all churches had to be re-consecrated. The sacred Tabots and Geez liturgy were to be discarded. Ethiopian saints were to be denounced and in many cases, their remains dug up and discarded. It was too much, and the revolt became a civil war. Catholics began murdering Ethiopian monks, and quickly there were armies of Ethiopians raised by opposing nobles, and religious leaders marching against King Susenyos. The leader of this uprising was Melka-Krestos. The struggle lasted for about ten years and finally ended when Susenyos finally convinced his men, who were reluctant to do battle with the rebels, to do so. They won the battle, killing more than 8,000, but were so appalled by what they had done to their fellow countrymen that Susenyos decided to drop the attempt to convert the country.

Fasiladas his son, who would succeed him, had this to say to his father: *"The men you see here strewn upon the earth were neither pagan nor Muslims…They were your own subjects, your compatriots, some of them your kinsmen…This is no victory that we have gained"….'* His father, seeing the irony of the situation, decided to end the conflict and abdicated in favor of his son. Before doing so he delivered a proclamation doing away with the evil oppression saying; *"Let the clergy return to the churches and set up their own altars for the Sacrament; let the people follow their own Liturgy, and may their hearts be glad."*

The Portuguese Return

History rates Susenyos as a very successful ruler even though his decision to convert the country to Catholicism did lead to turmoil and bloodshed for about ten years. He remained a Catholic, faithful to his conversion. Geez literature underwent a revival. It was during this period that some scholars say the Fetha-Nagast was compiled. Perhaps more important was the establishment of Amharic by the Catholics as a written language, useful for scholarly work. It was these activities and others like it that made this era known as the Renaissance in Ethiopia. Architecture, art, and literature underwent significant changes. Susenyos was also praised for civil reforms, social justice, and the splendor he introduced. In particular he was praised for the colorful parades of his Imperial Army. Doresse cites the official records that describe: *"The Imperial army procession, headed by the flag and kettle-drums with sword bearers and fusiliers marching before the holy image of Christ Crowned with Thorns...and always borne aloft into battle; next, the king and his escort of military generals, umbrella-bearers, and grooms with shields; and lastly in their serried ranks a multitude of infantry and horsemen."*

The Tents Come Down – Palaces Go Up –

This followed the religious crisis over the attempt of the Catholics to oust the Ethiopian Christians from control of the church. The Catholics were forced to leave their homes and seek sanction elsewhere, many going to Axum and some leaving Ethiopia. In spite of this activity, Fasiladas decided to abandon the tent capitol in favor of a fixed location, a palace in what became the city of Gondar. Axum had lost its influence years earlier when the Muslims had taken over Adulis, its principal port on the coast. Gondar was a few miles south of Lake Tana in the region of Gojjam and Begameder.

It was not a time of peace, but in spite of the fighting that seemed perpetual, it was a time for art and literature to thrive. Palaces, churches, and monasteries were built. Strangely, the unity of the country was falling apart as the princes and the lords feuded and fought for control. At the same time the emperor's court in Gondar was a very lively place. Doresse has this to say: *"It tells a story of life at court complete with hunting and ornamental gardens and every kind of pleasure in an entirely novel setting, of pious works extravagantly produced, of religion itself lost in the delights of subtlety.... In spite of a general decline, a number of outstanding personalities emerged, shrewd politicians and military leaders, empresses and princesses possessed of beauty, wisdom, patience and courage, by whose grace the milk of human kindness continued to flow despite the palace mutinies an assignations."*

The two emperors who followed Fasiladas were Yohannes and Yasu the Great. These two continued to have lively courts and to the extent possible ignored the struggles of the princes and lords going on outside Gondar. Churches, monasteries, and a library were built by Yohannes. Also he was a great believer in learning and promoted it along with theological debates. In spite of his intellectual proclivities, he found time for a series of forays against the Agaws and the Lastas, destroying their idols and temples. The first major structure in what was to become Gondar was the palace of Fasiladas, but other noteworthy structures soon followed.

Drawings - This is of some of major structures of Gondar as shown in the publication *A History of Ethiopia in Pictures* by Pankurst and last published by Oxford University Press, 1972.

The drawings: Beginning top left the castle of Empress of Mentaub, middle top row Emperor Iyasu with his mother Empress Waleta Giorgis and the last one top row the ruins of Qusquam Abbey just outside Gondar. The bottom row left the bath of Emperor Fasiladas, now used for the "Timkat" or Epiphany celebration, next on bottom row details of stone carvings from Qusquam Abbey, next on bottom row part of painted ceiling in Debra Birham Church, Gondar, next The exterior of the Derbra Birham Selassi.

Picture that I took in 1973 showing the palace of Fasiladas. My wife Agnes is standing in the door. Bath is in foreground.

More pictures of Gondar taken in 1973. The palace of Empress Walena Giorgis is in center back and that of Fasiladas is in right foreground.

This is the most elaborate of the palaces in Gondar. It is thought that builders from India designed it and with Ethiopian laborers built this palace. There were Portuguese in the country at this time capable of constructing this palace, but it is highly unlikely that they did as Fasiladas was busy driving them out of the country due to their trying to do away with the Ethiopian Church.

When my wife and I were living in Ethiopia we were told that the Italians, who occupied a part of Ethiopia for six years just prior to WWII, used some of these palaces as their headquarters during this period.

Yasu the Great

This was the last great emperor for the next one hundred and fifty years. He was very pious and orderly, fond of discussing religious matters, especially about the nature of Christ. He liked to go on hermitages to Lake Tana, restored several churches and built the sanctuary of Debra-Berhan 'Abbey of Light'. He was the only one able to open the sacred Ark in Axum. In addition to being renowned for his intellectual abilities, he was an excellent administrator. He revised the Fetha-Nagast (civil code) thereby improving many of the laws of the land. In addition, he found time to lead several expeditions against unfriendly tribes such as the Shankalla and Galla, defeating them soundly and taking many prisoners. Also he could be diplomatic when the occasion called for it. For example one Turkish Naib (chief) put a tax on some gifts that were passing through the port of Ariko. This offended Yasu, but rather than send his military in, he shut off the supplies that were being provided by the Ethiopians. The Naib promptly swore allegiance to Yasu and the problem was solved.

The Tents Come Down – Palaces Go Up ◈ ◈ ◈ ◈ ◈ ◈ ◈ ◈ ◈ ◈ ◈ ◈

Prosperity that marked the reign of Yasu was attributed to the flow of caravan traffic that flowed between Ethiopia and Eritrean ports at this time. He built a luxurious palace in Gondar, one not as large as that of Fasiladas but more spectacular. However, in spite of all his great deeds, he was ousted from control by his own son who wanted to rule before his father was ready to give up the throne. Yasu did abdicate and retreated to Lake Tana. But a few months later his son, fearing his father would take back the throne sent some assassins. A common soldier shot him and finished him off with a sword. The people who lived on Lake Tana were incensed by his death; especially that he was killed, as they put it, by a common soldier's hands. An extravagant funeral was held for him and thereafter he was considered to be a saint and martyr.

From Yasu the Great to Theodore (1700-1855)

This was a period of little progress in Ethiopia. For much of the time the various emperors were busy building palaces and churches in Gondar, and court intrigue. Art and writing received a boost during this period. For the most part, ambitious nobles were in control bringing emperors to the throne and deposing of them as they saw fit. As usual, the Galla of the Wollo area were on the move militarily. They were encouraged by the fact that they had managed to get one of their tribe on the throne, Wabi the Galla wife of Yasu II. Other areas of Ethiopia were also on the move such as Lasta that was defending its autonomy under the Zagwe dynasty, and Tigre where Ras Mikael was expanding his territory.* *Dorsee has provided the historical information in past sections.*

Physical Aspects

In order to have a good understanding of Ethiopia, it is necessary to know something about the uniqueness of the land. Some have described it as an impregnable fortress because of its location in rugged mountains with flat-topped plateau remnants. These remnants are known as ambas. The mountains are 15,000 ft. high in some places with extensive plateaus ranging from 6,500 to 10,000 ft. high. This region is now divided between Ethiopia and Eritrea and is said: "to provide the setting for unique developments of human culture...The rugged relief results in lands of diverse climate and agricultural potential being encountered within remarkably short distance. The high lands, according to Phillipson, result from, "tertiary earth movements accompanied by large-scale volcanism."

While the rugged mountains and high plateaus have served to protect Ethiopia from predatory foreign countries, especially the Italians, during the six years they tried to occupy the country, travel conditions have suffered. Give the Italians credit; they recognized the lack of decent roads was a major factor preventing their occupation of Ethiopia and were busy building bridges and roads when time ran out. They were forced out because they were on the losing side in WWII and had to give up in Ethiopia.

The primary rock types are granite and basalt. The soil type is volcanic and is reputed to have high inherent fertility. Erosion has likely caused the rugged topography. It is also responsible for depositing much soil in the Nile River that has been washed away from Ethiopia. Ethiopia suffers loss of much of its forest from human exploitation of wood to cook with. It seems to be little understood that if you consume the forest you have to replace it. Failure to replace the forest has lead to serious erosion and loss of land to gullies. Church land owners seem to be more conscious of the value of protecting and preserving the forest, and have in the Christian highland areas protected indigenous forest areas. In the nineteenth century, Australian Eucalyptus was introduced to Ethiopia and is now its most popular tree for reforestation and construction purpose.

Minerals are limited in Ethiopia. Early in its history it exported gold, silver, incense, and ivory. Its principal export is now coffee. I must mention that in 1973, when I was in Ethiopia, the Tenneco Corporation came to Ethiopia and explored for oil for about a year. No oil was found, or at least not enough to explore further. However, natural gas in sufficient quantity was found, but I do not recall that any commercial operations taking place at that time. This could have been due the political situation in that country at the time, a coup about to take place. Ethiopia does have another energy producing potential, a hydro-electrical plant on one of the several major rivers. I no longer recall the name of the project.

Most of Ethiopia's exotic animal population has become very scarce. I recall visiting a watering place in southern Ethiopia and none of the exotic animals (big game) that we go to Africa to see showed up, lions, tigers, elephants, giraffes, etc. I did not see these animals in the many other places I visited in Ethiopia. The introduction of firearms and the increase in population likely hastened the disappearance of these animals. All of this is not to say there are none of these animals in Ethiopia. There are reports that in some of the low populated areas of the south and west some big game animals can be found.

** The information in section Titled Physical Aspects is for most part from book titled, Ancient Ethiopia by David W. Phillips, published by British Museum Press in 1998.*

Cultural Aspects

In view of this rather uninteresting state of affairs in Ethiopia during the period from the late 1700s to 1855, I have elected to discuss some of the cultural history of this period. Before doing so, I should mention that Gondar was overcome at least a couple of times during this period and lost its significance as the capitol of Ethiopia. During this period monarchs lost their power and became more or less inconsequential. This period is known as the "era of the masafent or judges," a period of disunity and civil war, in the history of Ethiopia. An Ethiopian chronicler bemoaned "that kingdom had become contemptible to striplings and slaves and a laughing stock to the uncircumcised." The kingdom was no longer unified. The provinces were for the most part independent, ruled by the local lords. In this section I shall rely on Richard Pankhurst for much of the cultural historical information. *His recent book is entitled *"A social history of Ethiopia."*

Skilled Service Needs

As might be expected, the development of Gondar as a permanent capital required a large number of artisan, skilled laborers, builders, food vendors, and other skilled workers. Fortunately, there were a number of skilled foreigners in Ethiopia who could be used to train the relatively unskilled Ethiopian workers. I must say however, that the Ethiopians were still relying on foreigners to perform some of the more skilled task in that country when I was in Ethiopia in the mid nineteen seventies. I suspect their mindset was just not in the direction required to produce skilled workers, merchants, and other service providers. Certainly there were a very limited number of schools provided to train such people. I attribute much of this lack to the way the country was structured from the time of Axum as a dynasty with a divine right ruler, lords over peasants, and beneath the peasants the slaves.

Enterprising foreigners from Armenia seemed to have filled the mercantile sector in Ethiopia, particularly in the sale of jewelery including the designing and making, and clothing, furniture, and food marketing. The Muslims are also prominent in the merchant class. Ethiopians are the farmers. If you recall in our own country, agriculture employed over eighty-five percent of our working population, but now it accounts for less than five percent. The same is true in other progressive countries. Most of the problem with Ethiopia is due to its dynastic structure that precludes the freedom of its population to decide what is best for them. We call it democracy. Their middle class is small and unable to bring about the changes that are needed. The majority of the population has no idea as to what they could do if properly motivated and trained in what we call blue collar or service jobs. Ras Walda Sellase had this to say in 1811 "to Henry Salt; "that his co-religionaries were little acquainted with commercial transactions, as they dedicated their lives solely to war and agriculture, so that trade had rested from a very long time in the hands of Mahometans. One of the results of this was that merchants, like trade, tended, Consul Plowden stated, to be looked on with contempt by the military, though they were patronized by the chiefs whom the traders conciliated by rare presents..." Of course not all felt this way; there were a few who were wealthy Ethiopian merchants.

This statement from Ras Walda Selassse tends to support my position on lack of motivation. I can recall that a century or so ago British gentry looked down upon the merchant class in that country. To them it seemed a grubby profession, not worthy of their concern except when they needed money from them or their services.

The Ethiopians do better in professional jobs, especially in the government, political, teaching, and religious fields. This may be because the sons and daughters of the upper class have had the better opportunities to attend the best schools and to be educated abroad. As you will see in the next section, many people have elected to enter the religious field of work because it has enough prestige and promise to draw them. Later I shall be discussing the military as an occupation that has drawn many Ethiopians because of its better opportunities for them to move up.

I must observe that in nearly all of the other countries that I have worked in, some twenty five or more, where there is a dictator form of government and little or no opportunity for people to be free to vote there is not likely to be an effective middle class. When this is the situation, the better jobs are likely to be filled by foreigners, especially in the mercantile businesses. Liberia is a good example, where the Lebanese are the merchants. Kenya is another, where the Indians are the primary merchants.

Religious Influence

Because Ethiopia was a Christian Empire, a much larger portion of the nation's resources were devoted to building churches, monasteries, and hermitages than should have been. It was said by some Ethiopian historians that about twenty-five percent of the population was employed by the church. The following quotation provides a good idea as to population working in the church in Ethiopia. It is from Panhurst's aforementioned book on social history: "Observers of the early nineteenth century, as of previous times, were much impressed by both the multitude of churches and clergy. Ferret and Galinier remarked, in terms reminiscent of Bruce a century and a half earlier, that it was rare in the highlands to stop at the top of the mountain without seeing five or six churches and almost as many monasteries." Pearce likewise declared that priest were 'numerous beyond belief' while Dutton later in the century claimed that...innumerable priest and dabatras constituted nearly a quarter of the population. Most churches, according to Ferret and Galinier, "were tended by ten or twelve priest." In the larger churches this number could go as high as two hundred."

This high proportion of population, or misdistribution, working for the church caused numerous problems. For example, the excessive number required that a high percentage of the country's land belong to the church. Some estimates put the percentage as high as one-third. This was judged to be too high by those more favorably disposed to the Church, but even they admitted the percentage was high. Certainly there were some, described as soldiers of fortune who were seizing religious fiefs to give them to their followers. At other times some of the emperors were taking land from the churches.

Also this excessive number of priest and dabatras led to greed on their part. Quoting from Pankhust: "The hearing of confessions and granting of absolutions, was according to Pearce, a not unprofitable business." The average priest might moreover, have two or three thousand parishioners, each of whom would give him one or two amole, or one fifteenth of a Maria Theresa thaler...or a totalof 200 thalers a year. A priest after five or six years would thus have made enough money to maintain themselves for the remainder of their lives." It was observed that many would purchase oxen and then commence farming. It does seem these priests must have been greedy if they were able to retire after having worked only five or six years. Pearce and other such observers point out examples where the size of clergy's charges for bestowing blessings for a person's spiritual welfare, births, christenings, burials, and the like were abnormally high. Some likened them to locust. In spite of the fact that some of the clergy engaged in these questionable activities most were viewed favorably and were highly respected, influential, and politically powerful.

The Dabtaras sang in the churches and were paid for this service, but in addition some became legal advisors to provincial rulers. Of a more dubious nature, some made a living producing amulets, and charms against disease and misfortune. Some practiced medicine and claimed to have exorcising supernatural powers. Some claimed they could prevent the ravages of smallpox and destruction from locust and hail. Others were "hangers-on at some churches. Overall the Dabtaras were not very well thought of by most church members.

Cultural Aspects

The Traders

Over the centuries, beginning with Aksum in Ethiopia in the late centuries BC, the predominant traders have been Muslims. Pankhurst has devoted an entire chapter to this subject. It is, I might add, an interesting chapter. Here I have tried to present some of the most interesting aspects of his chapter.

Caravans – how they are organized and operate – has always fascinated me. They remind me of the wagon trains that played such an important role in the settling of our country. I think of some of our folk heroes like Daniel Boone and Kit Carson and how they safely led settlers through Indian country, the mountains and other obstacles in order to reach new lands. Of course trading was not their purpose, but many aspects of the caravans were similar. For example, the caravans had to be organized. A time was set for departure, a route, guides, and guards were selected. Most important, a leader must be chosen. One method of choosing a leader was for the traders to set up their tent on the first day, as close as possible to the most important trader. This trader automatically became the leader. Another method, and I believe the most common one, was for the traders to get together in a meeting and select a leader. I expect many of these leaders must have been paid for their services as their responsibilities were many. They chose the times of departure, when to stop, selected the camp sites, and were responsible for posting guards. Most importantly, they were responsible for settling disputes. But they did not in any way become involved the business deals of the merchants.

After Gondar was built in late seventeenth and early eighteenth centuries, it became a major trade center. One caravan route ran east to port at Massawa. Another began in Gondar and travelled west along the old western trade route to the Sudan and Egypt. Mainly slaves and ivory were exported to Egypt. In return spices, paper, brass, iron, brass wire, mercury, white and yellow arsenic, incense. Last but not least, a blacken substance (kohl) used by the ladies to blacken around their eyes and eyebrows. Based on my travels in Egypt, this substance was also much prized in that country. The Ethiopians did not like the Muslims but they valued them highly as trading agents. In Gondar, the Muslims were required to live in separate part of the city. Intermarriage was not allowed. Christians were not allowed to work for Muslims. This edict included Christian slaves. There were instances when some of the emperors would hire Muslims to represent them as their agents in business deals. Also the Armenians were highly valued and trustworthy as traders or agents.

Other aspects that deserve mention include the names of the major market centers; said to be Gondar, Adwa, and Aleyu-Amba. One large one that should be included is port city of Massawa, and of course there are many other smaller places – too numerous to mention – that operated markets. Some of the smaller places encouraged the caravans to stop and hold a market in their village or town by preparing camping grounds for them. Of course there was one stipulation, they expected the traders to buy feed and victuals from the residents.

I also found certain caravan protocol interesting, quoting: "In a typical caravan of the 1830's described by Ruppell the four richest merchants rode on mules; the rest walked on foot. Mules were used when the climbing was in the rocky or precipitous cliffs areas. These animals were sure footed and necessary when traveling in mountainous country These sturdy beast were moreover far from expensive…Traders crossing deserts or sandy regions…made use of camels These remarkable animals could carry no less than 350 kilos, or almost eight times as much as a mule, and could be fed on almost anything available, barley, beans, or brushwood, while existing for a week on a mere liter of water. There were finally human porters, many of whom could be found in Gondar, Adwa and other main towns The average porter travelled 20 to 30 kilometers a day and carried about 25 kilos, or about half as much as a mule, for two to three Maria Theresa thalers for a distance of 400 kilometers. Many merchants also employed their servants to carry loads, but slaves were better treated, for the master would reckon that they were worth 10 to 15 thalers per head, and if one died he would be the loser by that amount."

These caravans travelled well known routes and made market stops in towns and villages along the way. Some of these caravans would take as much as ten months to reach their final destination. Along the way they were required to pay a variety of taxes and charges as they passed through different areas. Caravan taxes were collected at custom post, and there were said to be eleven between Gondar and Massawa. Plowden noted that "custom houses…have been established on every spot where nature…has confined the road to some narrow defile, not to be avoided without an immense detour, if at all, and near some commanding elevation where a good lookout can be stationed at a brook fordable at one spot." Dues, which varied greatly from one kella (custom post) to another, were mainly paid in kind. Pepper to pay these levies was often used. As might be expected, the traders considered these taxes a source of inconvenience and irritation. This led traders to resort at times to smuggling to avoid these taxes, and of course there were frequent quarrels. At times it was necessary for the monarch to intervene in order to settle the disputes.

In addition to this taxation problem in some areas there were robbers who specialized in robbing caravans. Every caravan had guards to protect against such intruders. In some areas it was necessary to build thorn fences to keep out these thieves at night. I do not recall any band of thieves being reported in Ethiopia comparable to those that inhabitated Petra in Jordan about this same time. These thieves set up a village in a narrow gorge along a caravan route and made forays on caravans passing nearby, robbing them. They would then take refuge in their village that was so well protected by the narrow entrance it was virtually impossible to get to them. This lasted for years until the Romans who occupied that part of Jordan in those days grew tired of the robbers and sent and expedition of soldiers to Petra and took it over. Petra is one place you must see if you are sightseeing in Jordan.

Nobility

Elsewhere I have made brief mention of the nobility in Ethiopia. Here I shall go into more detail on the nobility. I don't recall that I have ever been in any country, including my own, that does not have some form of class system. I do, however, find it a bit strange to find such a complicated system as that in Ethiopia. It is not only complicated but varies from province to province as well. I am relying on Pankhurst, who has given the most consideration to this cultural sector, for my understanding. Even he seems to be having trouble understanding it. With these caveats I shall do my best to explain the Ethiopian nobility system.

As mentioned previously, Ethiopian rule was based on the divine right theory that originated with a child whose father was King Solomon and mother the Queen of Sheba. The child became Menelik I. This lasted until 1974, over 2000 years, when Emperor Haile Selassie was overthrown by a coup of junior army officers. The monarch (emperor) is at the top of the system and even when there is a weak monarch he seems to command considerable respect. At least outwardly this is the case. His commands may not be obeyed, but this is done in a circumspect way so as to not appear to offend him. It was customary for those approaching the emperor to prostate themselves before him, though there were times when the emperor would request the subject not prostate himself. Also one of the perogatives of the emperor was to appoint the governors of the various provinces. There were times when this power was stripped from the emperor by a potentate more powerful than he. Of course, the emperor expected the nobles to raise troops and turn them over to his command when requested. This was a measure of his strength. As long as the nobles respected his request he remained in control.

Mention has been made that when Gondar was built the monarchs quickly adopted it as Ethiopia's capitol. Roving capitols ceased. Monarchs and their courts liked the luxuries afforded by the palaces in Gondar. They continued to remain there even though their power decreased rapidly after the reign of Iyasu (1682-1706). "In the mid-eighteenth century, however, the Gondar monarchy finally disintegrated. The area under centralized control contracted, and the nobles usurped much of the powers formerly wielded by the monarch. The emperors became little more than puppet rulers."

Next in line were the nobles who held their titles subject to the whim of the emperor, except when the nobles were powerful enough to ignore the dictates of the emperor. These nobles received their titles from the emperor and they were not hereditary, except for those of the princes and princesses. Because the tiles were not hereditary it seemed they were used by the emperor to gain favors in the form of land and troops. These titles were evidenced by a headband of taffeta, bearing the name of the then monarch... and his title "Emperor of Ethiopia," of the Tribe of Judah....I recall there was one group of nobles who went by the title of Drummer. This title indicated that when they rode down the road drum beaters would accompany them.

Another practice I found a bit unusual was that of placing the unwanted princes of the royal families in a prison atop the tall mountains of Wehni. This practice began shortly after the capital was moved to Gondar with the reign of Emperor Fasiladas (1632-1667) onward. This continued until the Gondarine period ended. The obvious purpose of incarcerating these princes was to have them available when a vacancy occurred. They carried the proper blood line and this provided some assurance of their being available when needed. Of course, if they were left to fend for themselves, they might decide to assemble troops to overthrow the legitimate monarch. In any event, they were supposed to live under pleasant conditions, more like house arrest than prison. Unfortunately, this was not always the case. One of the emperors, Iyasu I paid his relatives a visit and found them living under some deprivations and substantially increased their revenues.

Agricultural Workers (Peasants)

Next in line came the peasants who tended the lands that were controlled by the feudal lords (nobles). By the time the nineteenth century had arrived, the agricultural population consisted of three main categories: peasants, farm laborers, and proprietors. I have some difficulty with the proprietor's category. To me this implies ownership and it is my impression the land belonged to the state (emperor).

The large majority of these categories were small proprietors and peasants and they constituted the "backbone of the nation." They bore the largest part of the taxation, and provided most of the troops when the lords raised armies for themselves or the emperor. In spite of all this hardship they bore up well and "appeared attached to their way of life." The laborers were fewer in number than the peasants and were paid a daily wage, usually in kind. They were diggers of the soil, wood-cutters, and grass-cutters. Some were paid in salt bars that amounted to about three Maria Theresa dollars a year.

Peasants made up the largest segment of the population in Ethiopia and were a most important economic sector. Aside from the slaves, they were poorest and most abused part of the population. They were subservient to the lords who controlled the land they lived on, and provided the seed to plant. They also extracted about seventy-five percent of what was produced. True, the usual contract between the peasants and the lords called for a fifty percent split. Most lords inserted a risk factor that called for the peasants to pay an additional twenty five percent. In addition the peasants were required to muster and fight when called to do so by their lord. In those days it seemed there was always fighting going on and one can only wonder when the peasants found time to cultivate their crops and tend their animals. I suppose it was fortunate that prior to the founding of Gondar Ethiopian agriculture was not commercialized. The call to arms came so frequently that it was well systemized.

Quoting from Pankhurst book: *Three proclamations were usually made before the monarch marched. The first Bruce recalls, was "Buy your mules, get ready your provisions, and pay your servants for after such a day, they that seek me here, shall not find me."* The second generally made a week or so later was, *"Cut down the Kantuffa in the four corners of the world, for I do not know where I am going."* Kantuffa was a thorny tree that was liable to get caught in a soldier's clothing. The third and last proclamation was, *"I am encamped upon the Angrab, or Kahha (i.e. the two rivers around Gondar); he that does not join me there, I will chastise him for seven years."* According to Bruce the reference to seven years relates to the Jubilee year of the Jews for whom seven years was a prescription for all debts and all trespasses.

These wars were often fought in the fields and villages where peasants lived. Their homes and crops would be destroyed, causing yet another hardship for them. Bruce the Scotchman, whom I have referred to a number of times, provides a particularly vivid description of one such example: *"On approaching the Blue Nile, through which the soldiers…had passed, he found that all the country was forsaken; the houses uninhabited, the grass trodden down, and the fields without cattle. Everything that had life and strength fled before that terrible leader, and his no less terrible army; a profound silence was in the fields around us, but no marks of desolation." A little further along however, Bruce found "the houses all reduced to ruins, and smoking like so many kilns; even the grass, or wild oats, which were grown very high, were burnt in long plots of a hundred acres…whilst not a living creature appeared in those extensive, fruitful, and once well inhabited plains."*

In spite of all the trials and tribulations undergone by the peasants, they bore them better than one would have expected. Pankhurst and the others who reported on peasant conditions recorded no peasant rebellions during these periods. Certainly, they were beset by enough problems. I feel certain their deep religious customs and convictions must have enabled them to withstand the vicissitudes.

The majority of peasants were engaged in the production of grain and cattle. With the advent of Gondar, the peasants began the production of vegetable and fruits to be sold in the city produce markets. There was no mention of any commercial agriculture until the city of Gondar was built. Prior to that period agriculture was a subsistence activity. The peasants produced for themselves. In addition, they produced for the lords who controlled the land and the soldiers were authorized to take what amounted to their pay from the peasant's crops and animal herds. In addition monarchs imposed a tribute program (tax) that allowed them to take as many as a 100,000 cows a year. There were reports of provinces competing to see which could collect the most cattle. To add to the peasant's burden, they were expected to provide food and lodging for travelers who came through their area. If the traveler had servants with him they also had to be taken care of. Beyond all these problems and nuisances, the peasants suffered from poor government and occasional locust attacks. With all this to contend with, it is understandable that there was little incentive for peasants to improve agricultural production. Oh yes, I forgot to mention that a peasant farmer was not allowed to kill one of his cows without first getting permission from the lord who controlled the land he operated.

Pankhurst made some comments on the way peasants dressed. As might be expected, they were not fashion plates. In fact the women wore a variety of clothes that ranged from smocks or shawls made from sheep or goat skins. The men wore clothing made of wild animal hides. Unmarried women went topless and men bareley covered their private parts. When the wind blew they were exposed. Of course as time passed, their dress became more prudent. Cotton clothing replaced some of the animal hides. In Ethiopia, as in other third world countries, change is not rapid, including clothing.

In my estimation, the peasants were being treated the most unfairly of any other sector of the economy. As mentioned, they make up the largest and most important sector of the economy. Were they to be treated properly and encouraged to produce up to their potential, the entire country would benefit. Before this can happen some of the elements necessary for a sound agriculture must be added.

This country is favored in manpower, water (lakes and rivers), land, and while the land is not the best it is certainly capable of producing crops. Also this land can be upgraded by use of fertilizer and other farm chemicals, and use of irrigation in certain areas. It also has some minerals such as gold and precious stones. Based on my contact with the Ethiopian people when I was over there, I found them easy to work with and train. Missing is an agricultural system that allows the farmers to own and control the land they live on. Also they are missing other parts of the present day agricultural institution such as a local marketing system, a credit system and extensions system to train farmers. It is my hope that the United States and other Western countries can gather again to provide technical assistance to this country. In 1974 this was happening, but unfortunately Haile Selassie, his family and a few others would not rid the country of decadent feudalism.

Miscellaneous Oddities

In my reading of Pankhurst, I came across a number of odd items worthy of mention. For example, there were some monks who did not eat bread, but existed on herbs such as water-cresses, water-parsnips, nettle, mallows, and kale. Alvares tried eating these herbs and found them miserable. He also reported that the eating of such foods by monks was rather commonplace. It was done as a sort of penitence.

Then there was another form of penitence, described as the mortification of the flesh, the wearing of an iron girdle with thick spikes to lacerate the skin. Also there were monks who on Lent would spend the entire day standing – some doing so in uncomfortable quarters wearing hair cloth.

There were priests, monks, and nuns who would immerse themselves in water for long periods as a form of penitence. They would crouch on stone in water up to their necks. This practice was prevalent throughout the land.

Circumcision of women was widely practiced in Ethiopia. It was not based on religion, but the clergy did, and still do defend it. It has been practiced in Ethiopia since ancient times. It is customary with Muslims, followers of Judaic type religion, non-Christian, and Ethiopian Christian women. It is performed by women but not by their choice. At some point in time men decided women should be circumcised (mutilated) in order to ensure the sex act would not pleasure them and cause them to be unfaithful. This procedure has been widely condemned by missionaries, and international civil rights groups for years, but this is one custom that seems to have a long life.

Ethiopia produces a mild narcotic that goes by Amharic name of chat or khat but is pronounced cat. It is a privet like weed that is chewed by users. It is unique to Ethiopia and is used by both men and women, often at social occasions. Sometimes men who engage in heavy labor will chew khat in order to give them an extra burst of energy that enables them to perform tasks that otherwise might not be possible. The extra energy lasts for two or three hours. After this period, the user will drink tea and then fall into a deep, somewhat hypnotic sleep. Chat is exported to nearby countries such as Somalia and Yemen.

Women

For the most part women were engaged in agriculture, handicrafts, and marketing of produce. Of course they spent great deal of their time about the kitchen. They were especially involved in the grinding of corn, a particularly burdensome task involving the use of two grinding stones. The task was so arduous that not even the slaves would grind corn. Another task they performed was the washing of clothes. They also gathered fire wood and carried water on their head. They made injera, the traditional food of Ethiopia.

There was a variety of dress among the women. As might be expected, dress varied based on age, marital status, and wealth. Married women covered themselves completely while those not married, prior to the Gondarine period, left their breast uncovered. However, they did decorate their breast with small beads. Upper class women dressed lavishly in silks and other fine clothes. The traditional garment for women was a loose-fitting garment known as a shama and usually made of cotton.

During periods when a war was going on, or the capitol was on the move, women became camp followers and had regular duties such as makers of the injera, taj, and talla. They did the grinding of the corn and carried along the food supplies.

Upper class women had servants, either slaves or peasants, to perform many of the task outlined above, but they were also camp followers. There was one emperor Zar'a Ya'qob (1434-1468) who became dissatisfied with two of his male officials and appointed his two daughters to take their places. He also appointed nine princesses to be governors of provinces. Education was restricted to males except in upper class families.

Women – particularly upper class women – had some rights not even available to women in Western Countries. One of these was the right to own land and other properties. According to Pankhurst this privilege appeared to become much more prevalent about the time Gondar was being developed beginning in the early 1600s. Examples were cited of women buying and selling land especially in the city of Gondar, the giving of estates, and providing land for churches to be built. Evidence of these transactions was found in the margins of numerous manuscripts.

Information that women or men were allowed to buy and sell land puzzles me. I was of the impression that all land belonged to the emperor and that he gave it to the lords, but there were no deeds or binding contracts. As has been noted, the monarchs ruled on basis of divine right. This gave them immense rights and authority. Pankhurst: *"that provincial rulers in his day were frequently appointed and dismissed, every two years, and sometimes every year, and even every six months....Fiefs seemed to be sold rather than given, for. No one receives them except by giving for them an amount of gold which is more or less the income and profit the aspirant and applicant hopes to get for them."* Almeida notes there are many applicants and the bids are often more than the Fiefs are worth. To recover their losses they overtax the peasants. Those selling the Fiefs – emperors and governors – appear to be more interested in the money to be made from the sales than in ruling properly. Of course not all monarchs and governors were as greedy as those described by Almeida. As in most situations of this nature there were some good and some bad. Unfortunately, there seem to have been more bad than good.

In researching the matter of land ownership in Ethiopia I ran across this statement: *"There is no single system of land tenure in Ethiopia, nor is there a simple means to determine ownership."* *- Hess. He also points out that some lands are held on a hereditary basis. Some is held by groups of villagers on a collective basis. As noted elsewhere in this document is that emperors have given land to various types of individuals, civil servants, military, and church groups. Also these emperors have generally reserved the right to take back these grants for various reasons. The land tenure system in Ethiopia results in numerous disputes, is very unsatisfactory and will be discussed further later. There seems to be no doubt that some women did own land and other property, and could have obtained it from governors or emperors.

Slavery

It is unclear when slavery first began in Ethiopia, but it was well underway by the sixteenth century. It was considered legal to have slaves in Ethiopia. It was provided for in the Fetha-Nagast or "Laws of the Kings" which declares that *"though all men were basically free, as God had created them, the law of war caused the vanquished to become the slaves of the victors."* The text goes on to sanction the taking of slaves from among the unbelievers (non-Christians). It also says the children born by the slaves shall belong to the owners in perpetuity. The Fetha-Nagast recognized that slaves were human, and possessed souls. Slaves who were Christians were to be provided facilities for worship. Non-Christian slaves were to be baptized. Christians were forbidden to sell slaves to non-believers. Taken these two requirements together meant that Ethiopian Christians were prohibited from selling slaves. Only the Muslims could legally sell slaves.

The Fetha-Nagast had other rules that suggested slaves be freed: 1) If a slave had served his master's father and grandfather; 2) If he had been baptized by his master and wanted to become a priest or monk; 3) If he had been made a soldier by his master; 4) If he had saved his master from death, had fought for him, or had protected him from mortal peril; 5) If his mother had been freed while he was in her womb; 6) If, after being taken prisoner in war, he returned voluntarily to his master; and 7) If his master died without heir.

Pankhurst reports that Alvares, a foreign traveler who has been mentioned previously, noted that the slaves in Ethiopia engaged in a variety of tasks. Large numbers of slaves plowed and sowed the royal lands. Some carried baggage, but a majority were employed in domestic service such as cooking and carrying firewood or water. Many slave women accompanied the army. The Muslims in Adal were frequently at war with the Ethiopians, and many of their prisoners were given to the Arabians in exchange for arms and horses. Also Alvares noted that slave prices varied considerably, depending on what part of the country they were being sold. It seemed that Ethiopian slaves were to be preferred over those from other African countries, especially in the nearby countries that have been mentioned.

During this period, it was reported that the Muslims seized many Ethiopian prisoners and sold them to the Arabians. Many of these slaves had been castrated before being sold as they brought more money when sold as eunuchs. One of the Amhara rulers at that time prohibited the practice of castration, declaring it an abomination. Some rebel Muslims continued the practice and there were reports that over half of those who were castrated died from the operation. Slaves from Damot in southern Gojjam were in particular demand and Portuguese priests reported that in Arabia, Persia, India, Egypt, and Greece there were many Ethiopian slaves.

It was reported that after the port of Massawa was seized in 1557, slave trading and raiding may have increased in the northern highlands. Baratii, an Italian traveler at that time, reported seeing Turkish soldiers returning to the coast with Christian slaves. And later in the 1700s) a Jesuit traveler, Teller, stated that "whenever the King of Janjero bought rare goods from foreign merchants he would give them in exchange ten, twenty, or more slaves, for which purpose he sent his people into any houses indifferently, to take away the sons of the inhabitants and deliver them to the merchants." He did the same when he presented slaves to persons of note.

Elsewhere the stealing of the sons and daughters of the peasants, as described in Pankhurst's book, was very audacious and cruel. Some were in the field herding sheep or other animals when stolen. Others were taken by raiders from the huts, night or day.

Some were taken from their bed while sleeping. It is difficult to understand how cruel people can be. The taking of children out of their beds and away from parents for purpose of enslaving them is too horrible to contemplate. Even worse, there were instances where children were sold into slavery by their parents.

One of the first emperors to protest against the slave trade was Emperor Susneyos (1607-1632). He forbade his subjects from dealing in slaves. He even had one of his subjects, a rich Muslim trader executed and his head stuck on a pole. It was placed in the market place as a warning. He then summoned his governors and ministers of court and warned them, under severe penalty, to enforce the law as required by the Fetha-Nagast. He cited the fact that large numbers of Ethiopian Christians were being sent to Arabia, India, Cairo, and Constantinople as slaves. This protest by Susneyos did not stop the slave trading. In fact, the Ethiopian rulers more or less ignored the Fetha-Nagast. When the capital moved nearer to the Sanqella territory in the western frontier area major raids were carried out during the reign of Fasiladas (1641-1659). They continued later by his son Yohannes I, and after that by Emperor Yostos. The Sanqella were mostly non-believers and black (Negroid) from the lowlands.

Of interest were the slaves who were used as soldiers by the Ethiopians and how they distinguished themselves. There was one group, described by Bruce as archers, who became important enough to influence the selection of emperor Bakaffa who was the successor to Dawit III. Unfortunately, this group of archers conspired against Bakaffa and were either banished or executed.

Another slave group reported by Bruce in the second half of the eighteenth century was those selected and trained as servants of the king and the nobles. These were usually young when selected – boys and girls in their late teens. They were instructed in the Christian religion and the tallest, most handsome, and best inclined were the only servants allowed to attend the king or lord in his palace.

The most important and distinguished group reported by Bruce, the Scottish foreign traveler, was the black cavalry, a force initially of about two hundred that increased to three hundred. They were commanded by foreigners and completely subservient to the king. According to Bruce *"the monarch when alone, took great delight in conversing with these slave warriors, and by strict attention their morals, by removing all bad examples from among them, and by giving premiums to those who read the most and best had made them in firmness and coolness in action equal perhaps to any of the same number in the world."* It seems that the greatest difficulty was in keeping them together because they were in such great demand by the lords as gate keepers. This was due to their impressive looks and discipline. They were also known for their reading ability because they had time on their hands and used it to read.

Based on what I was able to learn from Pankhurst and those foreign travelers whom he quoted from time to time about the slave situation, it was much better to be a slave in Ethiopia than in our country. They were better treated, did not have to make the long ocean voyage to America, and even though they were slaves, they never had to leave Africa and familiar surroundings. However, slavery lasted much longer in Ethiopia and in other parts of Africa than in America and most other places in the world. Several Ethiopian emperors tried to abolish slavery but were unable to do so until Haile Selassie did in 1923. At that time he was negotiating to become a member of the United Nations, and there was no way Ethiopia would be able to get in as a slave holder state. To be fair to Haile Selassie he likely used the maneuver to get in the United Nations as an excuse to rid Ethiopia of slaves. A primary use for slaves in Ethiopia was as household servants. Most of the slaves were owned by upper class Ethiopians and they were most reluctant to part with them.

Skilled Workers

In addition to those associated with agriculture, there are other segments of society that have not been discussed. For example there were handicraft workers, weavers, tailors, and pottery and ironware makers. There were also blacksmiths, goldsmiths, and silversmiths. Because of myths, old wives tails, and oral tradition passed on by Jesuits, the blacksmiths and other smiths were regarded with fear, distrust, and sometimes hatred. Ethiopians looked upon the smiths much as New Englanders looked upon witches back in colonial days. If a person who had been around a blacksmith came down with some form of illness and died, his relatives would blame it on the blacksmith and would often kill him. It must have had something to do with the fire, smoke, and fumes. It is possible that the Ethiopians may have associated the blacksmiths with the devil and his home, hell, seems strange. It was somewhat the same way with the witches of New England, though they rode a broom. Guess we can't be too critical of the Ethiopians.

Priest displays some handicraft items he uses in church services.

With all the religious activities that went on in Ethiopia, there had to be much ecclesiastical handicraft work. Some of the church establishments were wealthy and needed a wide variety of religious handicraft items such as crosses, basins, bells, chandeliers, robes, turbans, ceremonial umbrellas, church paintings, icons, scrolls, fine curtains, and tents. Most of the metal items were made of gold and silver.

Another type of handicraft, a one string Ethiopian type violin being played at a wedding ceremony in Addis Ababa, 1973.

Besides the handicraft work there was an out flowing of painting taking place in Ethiopia. Much of it was centered in Gondar. I came across an appointment calendar that my wife had picked up and saved when we were in Addis Ababa more than thirty years ago. In looking it over I discovered it was filled with copies of some of the more famous art work of the Gondar and pre-Gondar periods. Along with each picture, pertinent commentary presented. I have included some of these paintings here along with the commentary. The pictures have been divided into Pre-Gondar and Gondar periods. For example, Eve was painted in the Pre-Gondar period; Satan was painted in 17th century and is included in the Gondar period.

Equestrian saints are another new subject to appear during the second Gondarene period. Among these are: George, Mercurios, Demetrius, Claudius, Fasiladas, Susenyos, and others. The dragons speared by the various saints have different forms. Some are plain and some are in the form of men. The dragon associated with St. Susenyos is in the form of a woman. The monster Barzella who cast the evil eye on people and some are of semi-human form. St. Mercurios is generally spearing a dragon in the form of a man.

A particularly beautiful example of painting in the second Gondarene style, this plate shows a portion from a very large canvas painting which formerly was in a church in Lalibela dedicated to St. Mercurios. The canvas (figure 1) is composed of three main sections, the center depicting the virgin, with St. George on her right, and St. Mercurios on her left. Astride his customary black horse, St. Mercurios is conceived here as a young Ethiopian prince dressed in rich robes like those worn by the Negus and the nobility. Behind him is a figure and in the entrance to the gate of the city towards which he is riding are two priests holding hand crosses. Although restoration work has been done

Figure 1. St. Mercurious, National Museum, Addis Ababba, Seventeenth Century.

on the canvas, the empty space at the horse's feet no doubt at one time contained a dragon – perhaps in the form of a man. This painting is a distinctly Ethiopian expression even though some Western influence is evident. The bouffant hairstyles, the large dark eyes, the brocade robes so favored by painters of this time, and the horse's harness with bells – all are locally inspired. The drawing is unusually sensitive and the colors are more delicate, although this may be due in part to fading. Backgrounds are now being broken into different color areas – a device used primarily to isolate and intensify the subject matter.

Figure 2.

The next plate (figure 2) shows the center panel of a triptych which is in the church of Golgotha Mikael at Lalibela. A glance at the simplicity of its design recalls an earlier period in painting. However, the brocade robe, the break-up of the background colors, and the shading or modeling of the flesh areas are indications that this belongs to the Gondarene period. Part of the charm of this picture lies in its refreshing individuality. This is due mainly to the fact that the subject matter applies only to Ethiopia, and since there was no model, the artist was free to invent as he chose. King Lalibela is depicted seated on a simple wooden throne while around him are smaller figures illustrating the various miracles attributed to him by tradition.

Lalibela was a king of the Zagwe dynasty which had usurped the throne from the Solomonid Dynasty around 1100 A.D. Their most well-known achievement was the construction of the seven monolithic churches in the capital city of Floha. Tradition ascribes these remarkable churches to Lalibela who ruled from about 1190 to 1225, after which the town of Floha was renamed Lalibela.

And while scholars give a rather worldly account of Lalibela and the building of the churches, tradition offers this delightful version: At the time of Lalibela's birth a dense cloud of bees surrounded him. His mother, seeing this, cried out, "The bees know that this child is king." Accordingly, he was given the name Lalibela which means "the bee recognizes his sovereignty". He grew to be such an exceptionally handsome man that everyone said that he was destined to be king. When the reigning king, who was Lalibela's brother, heard of this prophecy he grew jealous and tried to poison young Lalibela. However the poison only rid him of tapeworm and produced a death-like sleep during which God showed him the churches in heaven which he was to build. When Lalibela's time came, God appeared to the king commanding him to abdicate in favor of Lalibela. When construction began on the churches, a company of angels worked with the men during the day and by themselves at night. Each day when the men arrived to begin work they were amazed to find that three times as much work had been accomplished as when they'd left the previous day. The men didn't know that the angels were helping them since they couldn't see them Lalibela knew because, due to his virtue, the angels didn't hide from him.

Figure 3.

Nearly all of the early artwork of Ethiopia was about religion and much of it was produced by the clerics and monks.

From the same Church of the Trinity as the preceding plate, Satan (figure 3) is another new subject and was introduced into Ethiopia by the Jesuits in the preceding century. Satan, who is also called Mastema or Diablos, is shown here engulfed in flames, bound in chains. He has large glaring eyes, horns, claws, three ears and wings. In the background are two serving devils, having snakes for tails and who attend two separated groups of bound men and women. The portraying of large groups of figures by means of a series of superimposed heads is characteristic of this painting style. A small head protrudes from between Satan's clenched teeth and relates to a legend which goes something like this: Once when Satan was roaming the earth – as he is allowed to do every thousand years – a girl saw him and fell in love with him. When she died she longed to see him so much that she asked God to forgive Satan and bring him to heaven. God sent the girl to hell, and when Satan heard of her request to God on his behalf, he put her between his teeth – from which position she was condemned to watch the horrors of hell for all eternity.

Ethiopian demonology was similar to that of the Christian or Egyptian Copts. They in turn had inherited many of their belief in devils and evil spirits from their ancestors, the so-called Pagan Egyptians. They believed in a personal devil that was able to take any or every form at will and could travel through earth, air, and water. He could assume the form of an ordinary individual and transact business with people, especially in the matter of buying their souls from them.

Missing a Foundation for Government

As mentioned earlier, the period from the early 18th century to the mid 19th century was defined by disruption and rebellion. Gondar as a center for central government was largely ignored. The various provinces were ruled independently by lords. The idea of a unified central government disappeared.

What went wrong? One answer might be that there were no strong contenders for the position of emperor during this period. The fact that there have been other times when emperors were weak and ineffective, suggests that this is not a sufficient answer. No, there are other answers. To begin with, the foundation for a central government is missing. Why is a central government needed? How should it be formed? What are the rules for transferring power? How should it be structured to rule? How should it be financed? These and other such matters are spelled out in the constitutions of developed countries. This has not been done in a satisfactory way in Ethiopia. True, it has the Fetha-Nagast, but as I understand it, is more of a history than a constitution. Lack of this causes instability, uncertainty, unfairness, and leads the strong to take unfair advantage of the weak. Conditions finally reach a point where chaos takes over. The citizens then realize they need help but they are not always sure how to get it. This is, in my opinion, what government is about. It is an effective method to marshal the intelligence and resources of the masses to solve problems for the common good.

It is well known that one the most powerful driving forces of human nature is self preservation, and that greed is an important component of that force. Greed (selfishness) is the driving force of the Capitalist system that the United States depends upon. Quoting Max Lerner in his introduction to Adam Smith's The Wealth of Nations: *First, "Smith assumes that the prime psychological drive in man as an economic being is the drive of self interest. Secondly, he assumes the existence of a natural order in the universe which makes all individual strivings for self interest add up to the social good."*

Coincidentally, Smith arrived at this fundamental truth when he was endeavoring to understand how to combat the feudalistic system, prevalent in Western Europe in his time. This happened to be the same problem that was causing the peasants to be so poor and downtrodden in Ethiopia. Unfortunately, the Ethiopians did not have the good fortune to have an Adam Smith and other learned social thinkers to tackle their economic problems.

Missing a Foundation for Government ◈◈◈◈◈◈◈◈◈◈◈◈◈◈◈

A comment about Adam Smith's theory and how it relates to Ethiopia's lack of a foundation: As we now know, his theory of competition was quickly accepted by the capitalist. It was justification for their position that government had no right to interfere with their business dealings – the less government the better. Fortunately, Franklin D. Roosevelt did not agree. Since his day, government has instituted some checks and balances on oppressive business practices. Some would say yes, but not enough. In fairness to Smith he never visualized a business world such as we now have. The competitive system that controlled his business world was atomistic; no business was large enough to be monopolistic. Smith was an advocator for the good of the people of the nation.

We now come to the four emperors who seemed to realize the need to create a more unified government for Ethiopia. These four followed the period when nobles were in charge and there was little attempt to run Ethiopia on a unified basis.The first of these was Tewodros (1855-1868), followed by Yohannes IV (1869-1889), Menelik II (1889-1913), and then Haile Selassie (1913-1974). Haile Selassie ruled as regent from (1913-1930).*

* *For factual information on Tewodros I have relied upon Pankhurst and Doresee.*

These two historians were pretty much in agreement on the personality of Tewodros – creative, harsh, and determined. Also they were in agreement on his major ideas for change. Doresee summarized his ideas in about three pages, whereas Pankhurst used a whole chapter on Tewodros. I must say that Doresse viewed Tewodros as perhaps more violent than Pankhurst. Both viewed him as eccentric. I have elected to use Pankhurst's list of reforms attempted by Tewodros:

1. **Unification and curtailment of feudal power.** Before he could become emperor, it was necessary to defeat the feudal lords who opposed him. Once this was done he wanted to unify the country by use of soldiers. He would place trusted officers over soldiers in the different provinces in place of lords. In effect, generals would rule subject to his command. This was a difficult task that would take a long time. It was not accomplished during his reign.

2. **Establishment of a standing modern army.** He was aware that effective armies did not rely on looting peasant farming operations for food and pay, especially the farming operations of his own people. He set about teaching his soldiers some discipline, forbade them from looting peasant lands, and began to pay them money for their services. He also set up granaries for the troops. He had a British officer train some of his soldiers, but the soldiers did not take kindly to the strict discipline and all the marching and saluting. The plan had to be abandoned.

The reign of Tewodros was characterized by much fighting. He realized the country was not unified. It would be necessary to conquer several of the rebellious regions and he set about to do so. His methods were often cruel – villages burned, crops pillaged, cattle slaughtered, and looted, and worst of all many innocent peasants were killed. One example of how Tewodros operated is quoted by Stern, a foreign observer in Pankhurst's book: Stern describing Tewodro's expedition to Wollo in1856 states: *"The villages were burnt, the fields laid waste, and men, women, and children were unsparingly butchered, or dragged into irredeemable captivity."* It was noted that later expeditions were no less destructive. Rassam, another foreign observer writing of a similar incident in Diambeya in 1866: He observed: *"Only two years before this district was in a most flourishing condition, every foot of it was under cultivation and a succession of villages dotted the length and breadth of the plain. Since that time, however, the area has become almost desert owing to the King's continued oppression of the poor inhabitants...only a field here and there appeared to be under tillage, and the villages-small groups of miserable huts – were few and far between, while the bulk of the inhabitants were said to have died of hunger and disease."* This region was revisited soon after and soldiers took everything they could lay hands on, including all the cattle.

This terrible destruction was all justified by Tewodros as acts to conquer the various regions resisting his rule. It worked and the country seemed to operate, but on and uneasy basis. He wanted to do good, but short of using excessive measures, did not have what was required. His goal of establishing a modern army was not achieved.

3. **Another need perceived by Tewodros was to make it safe to travel in the country.** There were bandits and an excessive number of internal custom posts interfering with this objective. He rid the roads of bandits by having a large group of professed bandits assemble under a false pretense and then killing all of them. He directed that the number of internal post be decreased to three but this decree was not strictly obeyed. Upon death of Tewodros it was discontinued.

4. **Tewodros perceived of a need to promote more technology in Ethiopia.** He considered sending Ethiopians to western Europe for training, but instead decided to import foreigners to train Ethiopians. He wanted to establish a modern army and he knew the major requirements were guns, rifles, and cannons. Of course he might have bought them, but he decided on making them.

He set about bringing in the experts, a group of missionaries proffered by the Anglican bishop of Jerusalem. First there were three Swiss Germans trained at the Pilgrim's Mission at St. Chrischona near Basle in Switzerland. These three were joined three years later by two colleagues. These missionaries were located at Gafat, a place that soon became the site of a royal workshop and arsenal. Eventually other Europeans settled there. The missionaries opened a school at which they taught handicrafts in addition to reading, writing, and religion.

Gafat soon attracted other technically minded foreigners who had come to Ethiopia independently. One of these was a Polish Jew who was said to have deserted from the Russian army. Others were a French gunsmith, a compatriot, and a metal worker. Then there was a German scientist, a renowned botanist. All of these foreigners worked together fairly harmoniously. They served as smiths, carpenters, engineers, saddlers, carriage builders, armourers, and manufacturers of cannons. They were reported to be hard working and produced a powerful water wheel to power different kinds of machinery.

Tewodros now had some technicians and he wanted some cannons made. This required a foundry in which to forge and cast the cannon. Iron ore and lime were available, but the ore had to be heated at a high temperature – 700° centigrade. Lest we forget, these technicians had never been trained to produce cannons or even to build a furnace. Fortunately, a French metal caster by the name of Jacquin, agreed to attempt the building of cannons if Tewodros would have the other craftsmen at Gafat assist him. Immediately a letter was written to head of the missionaries ordering them to assist Jacquin "in every way, to support him with advice and action, and to serve him as translators". The work was undertaken. A blast furnace was built and bellows were installed. The work of hauling the ore and lime was undertaken, the furnace fired up, and the bellows put to work. Unfortunately, the furnace melted before the iron ore. The Frenchman was overcome, nearly went mad and asked the Emperors permission to leave. Permission was granted.

The events that followed demonstrated the tenacity of the Emperor. He showed up at Gafat and swore by his death the cannon project should not be given up. The missionaries protested that if it were in their power to build the cannon they would do so. They stated that they were willing to do anything else they were qualified to do, but making cannons was beyond their ability. To demonstrate their sincerity, they made a gunstock – an item they knew the king (emperor) was interested in. The king was elated and immediately rescinded an order he had issued that all servants be taken from the missionaries. Then the missionaries working under the direction of the Polish Jew managed to cast a small mortar and some bullets. The king jumped for joy and thanked God, but immediately wanted a larger mortar. The Polish Jew protested, but agreed to try if the missionaries would help him. Again orders to help were given to the missionaries and this time after much labor and some failures the desired mortar was produced. The Ethiopians in the area who witnessed the new mortar were impressed and congratulated the Polish Jew and his crew of missionaries. This time the king's joy knew no bounds. He fervently thanked God and offered those who had made the mortar anything they wanted – short of his crown. He did give them a handsome amount of money and provisions for their households. It was not long thereafter that he asked them to make an even larger mortar; and they did.

The king was obsessed with the idea of equipping his army with muskets and cannons. He sent envoys to Britain with a request for more skilled workers and all kinds of weapons. This request was ignored and probably contributed to the breakdown of peaceful relations between Ethiopia and Britain that later occurred. In the meanwhile the Polish Jew and his missionaries continued to make more weapons even though they would have preferred not to do so. They knew the king wanted to put them all in chains and put them in prison but did not because they were making weapons. Because of the drive and the tenacity of the king he succeeded in building the first significant arsenal of artillery in Ethiopia. There were twenty-four brass cannons, four cannons, and nine brass mortars. The nine mortars were all built in Ethiopia.

5. **Road building:** Tewodros recognized that a strong military needs good roads and set about to improve them. Again he called upon the Protestant missionaries for help. He wanted to create a road network that would link Dabra Tabor with Gondar, Gojjam, and Maqdala. Tewodros showed his helpers how to build a road by doing manual labor in the construction process and working from early dawn till late at night. With his own hands he removed stones, leveled the ground, or helped fill up small ravines. Of course the workers did not dare to quit working as long as the king was working, nor eat or drink. A road that would have been credible in Europe was built. Moreover the craftsmen built a carriage, the first one in Ethiopia, for the king to ride in.

6. **Next the King thought about building a fleet of boats on Lake Tana.** He wanted to establish a small navy. His craftsmen again pleaded a lack of ability

and the king again persisted. This time, as he had done with the road building he physically went to work and made an immense flat bottomed bulrush boat of great thickness. He next constructed two large wheels that would be propelled by hand. It was, in fact a paddle wheel steamer minus the locomotive part. He built two more of these boats sixty feet long and twenty feet wide mid ship. They had wooden decks powered with two paddle wheels operated by hand much like a grindstone. About a hundred men were loaded aboard each and members of the British diplomatic mission were invited to witness the original trial. At first all went well and the king was mightily pleased. He then decided to test the boats in the wind and the first strong breeze revealed unanticipated technical problems and the boats began to fall apart. The king quickly decided to head for the shore. The project ended and before it could be begun again the king's untimely death ended it.

7. **The abolition of slavery was a priority of the ruler**, and had been since before he took over control of Ethiopia. As soon as he was in office he issued orders that slave exports in Ethiopia were to be abolished on pain of severe punishment. Unfortunately, like Emperor Susenyos who was opposed to slavery he did not have any way to really enforce his decree. Realizing this he decided to permit existing slaves to be sold to Christians, provided they were purchased for charity. He set an example by purchasing slaves and then baptizing them. He later decided against doing this and issued another order that anyone found selling Christian slaves would have his right hand and left foot amputated. Foreign observers were convinced that Tewodros was sincerely opposed to slavery. Of course this order did not result in the abolition of slavery. As previously mentioned it lasted until Haile Selassie's reign.

8. **Land reform was also on the king's list.** He proposed to institute laws to strengthen land tenure rights. He decreed that land should belong to those whose fathers had held it as fiefs. The decree was initially acclaimed, but it soon developed that every one claimed to have had a father with a fiefdom. The king had to reinstate the old institutions.

The king's attempt to change land reform institutions caused the priests in the province to press for the distribution of more land. It seems that some of the land formerly held by thechurch had been taken by the government, but the king thought that church already had more than its share. There was a flare up and some of the priests suggested that the king should "follow the time honored practice of marching from place to place in order to

> spread the burden of his court and army over the whole empire." The king was not amused and lashed out at the church. The army at first sided with the king against the Abuna and the priest. This dispute took place early in Tewodro's reign and based upon advice from faithful advisers, who reminded him that the people and the army were with the priest. He heeded this advice and the storm abated, but he still believed he was correct. He bided his time until 1860 and then introduced his church spoliation plan (church land appropriation). He also limited the number of priest who could be assigned to a church to 5 or 7 in the case of a large church. His plan was drastic. He confiscated all the church lands and revenues including some of the Abuna's own property. Of course the church was extremely disturbed and the king's offer to look after their material needs did not mollify them. They would not be slaves dependent on royal bounty. The Abuna's anger knew no bounds.

King Tewodros had other commendable goals that he tried to implement that are briefly summarized here. He opposed the lax sexual mores of his time and he, as head of the government, spoke out against them. He remained faithful to his first and second wife. His first wife died and he married a second time. He implored his people to follow his example of being faithful to his marriages. He was not pleased with the dress code and implored his people to wear loose flowing clothes instead of the half naked costumes that were customary with the Oromos.

He wanted to establish a more efficient communication system and to this end early in his reign took steps to substitute letters for verbal messages. He was aware of the cultural decline taking place in his country and set about to collect a great library of Ethiopian manuscripts, said to be the finest ever assembled.

A most important decision taken by Tewodros at the beginning of his reign was to abandon Gondar in favor of the mountain fortress of Maqdala. He not only abandoned Gondar but on two occasions, 1864 and 1866 attacked and virtually destroyed it. It had ceased to be the capital for any centralized government for over a century when Tewodros destroyed it.

Most of his efforts at reforms failed after he became angry with the British over its failure to reply to his request to come to his aid against the Muslims. He thought that because Ethiopia was Christian country as was Britain and that it would come to the aid of his country. His letter requesting aid was directed to Queen Elizabeth proposing a detailed alliance. He did not know that Britain had just concluded a treaty with Turkey against Russia and this made it difficult for Britain to aid a country that was not friendly with the Turks. He imprisoned the British Consul and some other Europeans. Tewodros was adamant and refused to free the British consul and the others. The British sent a military expedition under Sir Robert – later Lord Napier – to free the imprisoned Consul and other Europeans. Napier captured Makdala and on April 13, 1868 Tewodros committed suicide. Pankhurst noted that, *"opposition from the priesthood nonetheless seems to have contributed significantly to Tewodro's troubles and ultimate fall."* Because of some of his inhumane treatment of peasants and other Ethiopians the British forces were actually aided by some of the natives when Lord Napier attacked Maqdala. No mention was made of any suicide messages and so it is matter of conjecture as to exactly why he committed suicide.

Tewodros was highly creative, industrious and in some ways well meaning. He left a number of markers for those who followed him. In particular, his desire to professionalize the army was noteworthy. Attempts to improve communications included road building and written word record keeping in place of oral presentations. Also his efforts to unify the country were impressive. He recognized that excessive land holding by the priest was a problem needing attention. He was not very diplomatic. Too often he used the military when it would have been better to have used diplomacy. He was excessive in the destruction of homes, crops, animals, and people, especially when some of these were his own people. Certainly, he was an interesting but puzzling emperor, and in ways ahead of his time.

Yohannes IV and Menelik II

Yohannes IV was a prince of Tigre at time of Tewodro's death, and Menelik II was king of Shoa. Both had legitimate claims to rule as emperor of Ethiopia. Tewodro's unexpected death left many unfinished problems, most important being who would take over as ruler. The usual dance (warfare) to see who would take over ensued for several years and Yohannes a Tigrean prince emerged as the victor and was crowned Emperor Yohannes IV. He continued to pursue some of the same goals as Tewodros, containing the nobility and laying the basis for a modern state. As with Tewodros, *"struggles with regional lords, Europeans, and Sudanese Muslims prevented him from achieving his goals."* *

 * *Information on Menelik section is from book by Robert L. Hess, titled Ethiopia-subtitle modernization of autocracy.*

Even though Yohannes was crowned, there was another rival for the throne. Menelik the King of Shoa could claim Solomonic descent and had the loyalty of a large percent of the population, as did Yohannes. Fortunately before the rivalry could warm up, a truce was arranged whereby Yohannes agreed to have Menelik as his successor to the imperial throne. This arrangement was sealed when the son of Yohannes married the daughter of Menelik II. This truce was not long in effect before it was put to test by the Italians. They had established a foothold on the coast of the Red Sea by purchasing a small piece of land at Assab, suitable for a port. Next they took over the port of Massawa and from there moved to the border of Tigre. Here the Italians were met by the emperor's general, Ras Alula, in the battle of Dogali in 1887 and soundly defeated them.

To recoup, the Italians decided to resort to diplomacy by taking advantage of the tenuous relations between Yohannes and Menelik. Menelik knew Yohannes was well armed and that he was not. This meant Yohannes, in spite of the truce, had a chance to become the imperial emperor of Ethiopia. To prevent this, Menelik II concluded a treaty with Italy. Hess (historian) noted this was made possible by the failure of Yohannes to unify Ethiopia.

About this time Yohannes discovered another enemy facing him to the west – another religious sect – the Mahdist who had replaced the Turks and Egyptians in the Sudan. At the same time Yohannes saw this as an opportunity to expand his country to the west. That area had prospects of gold, slaves, and direct access to the Nile. Unfortunately for Yohannes, he was killed by a Mahdist bullet. This put Menelik II on the throne earlier than he might have been.

Yohannes IV and Menelik II

The historian Hess points out that the first Europeans in Ethiopia were generally travelers and missionaries. By the middle of the 19th century, Africa (including Ethiopia) was becoming of interest as potential colonial possessions. A wave of European imperialism had begun. Tewodros, we recall, used missionaries to build cannon, but now the Europeans were beginning to use Africans for their purposes. The Italians had their sights on the Ethiopians. Prior to this it had been, and still was, the Muslims who wanted to occupy parts of Ethiopia – particularly the coastal and adjacent inland areas.

Menelik II was now to bear the burden of preventing this incursion by the Italians; in fact he could see the need for help from them to add territory to his country. Menelik, upon becoming emperor, quickly signed the famous treaty of Uccialli. He hoped it would help to become a special friend of Italy, but the Italians interpreted the treaty as giving them the right of a protectorate over Ethiopia. *"Since 1885 they had hoped to obtain from the Sultan of Zanzibar the southern part of Somalia as an avenue of penetration inland to the rich lands of Kaffa, Sidamo, and Borana, then independent countries lying to the south of Shoa. In 1889 they proclaimed to the rest of the world that the treaty of Uccialli gave them a legitimate protectorate over Ethiopia. They did not realize at the time the considerable discrepancy between the Italian and the Amharic versions of the treaty".* Hess.*

Menelik expecting the Italians to aggressively pursue their claim, decided to impose his authority over an area much larger than any prior Ethiopian emperor had claimed in almost four hundred years. In addition to occupying the traditional lands of Gojjam, Begemdr, Amhara, Tigre, and Shoa, he also took over the newly won lands to the east around Harar. His armies scored even greater victories when they occupied the Somali country within 180 miles of the Indian Ocean. At the same time, other Ethiopian armies went south to destroy the ancient kingdom of Kaffa and to conquer Sidamo, and the Galla Borana area. These additions brought Ethiopia to about its size at beginning of twentieth century. For awhile after WWII it did have Eritrea.

Of course the Italians did not take Menelik's moves without a challenge. At the battle of Adowa on March, 1896 they were soundly defeated. Hess says, *"Ethiopia's independence was secured, Ethiopian prestige was unique on the African continent, and Italy was so embittered by defeat on the battleground that forty years later Italians still sought revenge for Adowa."*

When I was in Ethiopia in 1972-74, the Adowa victory was still being celebrated. I seem to recall it was celebrated as a national holiday each year on its anniversary. Furthermore, no other African country up to that time had defeated a western power. Ethiopia came out of the shadows into the limelight. Even the western countries took special notice of Ethiopia after Adowa.

It was Menelik who set up Addis Ababa as the new capitol of Ethiopia. It was he who had doubled the size of the country in a relatively short time, and who realized it was time to introduce new measures to modernize the government. It was Menelik who knew that he would need help from the western countries to modernize his government. He set about to locate and bring this help in. The Western powers, one after another, began to send in delegations to help with suggestions for change and to attempt to influence Menelik in their favor. Each was trying to extract concessions like those obtained by Europeans throughout the colonial world. According to Hess and other historians, Menelik was a worthy diplomat and was able to get more than he gave. The railway from Djibouti to Addis Ababa that was negotiated with France is one example. He granted a concession to France to build the railway and France provided the capital. He worked with Europeans to establish telecommunications, roads, technical assistance, and advisers. Menelik responded favorably to a request from President Theodore Roosevelt to establish official contact with Ethiopia and a consular officer with staff came to Addis Ababa in 1904 (see article on this visit that follows). I am not certain where I obtained this copy, but my recollection is that Bob Caldwell, a dear friend and a Labor attaché to Ethiopia, provided it to me.

Robert Skinner's unpublished account of the First American Diplomatic Expedition to Ethiopia

By Richard Pankhurst

At the turn of the present century United States interest in Ethiopia was aroused by the considerable sale in the country of American cotton goods. The U.S. Consul in Marseilles, Robert Skinner, proposed that a diplomatic mission be despatched to Addis Ababa, and in 1903 was commissioned by President Theodore Roosevelt to negotiate a commercial treaty with the Emperor Menelik. The mission left Marseilles in October of that year, reached the French Somaliland port of Jibuti on November 17th, and arrived in Addis Ababa on December 18th, the treaty being in due course signed on December 27th.

Skinner subsequently wrote two descriptions of the mission. The first was in his book *Abyssinia of Today. An Account of the First Mission sent by the American Government to the Court of the King of Kings* (1903-1904) which was published by Edward Arnold in London in 1906. The second account which never appeared, was conceived as Chapter III of an autobiographical study entitled " Recollections of Life in the Foreign Service of the United States."

This chapter, now made available through the kindness of the Consul's nephew, Mr. C. W. Skinner, and of Mr. James Bennett Childs, is, of course, much shorter than the book *Abyssinia Today*, but contains significant observations and remarks not included in that volume. Of particular interest are the descriptions of Ras Makonnen, father of Emperor Haile Selassie, Skinner's conversation with the Emperor Menelik on the *tabot* or " holy of holies ", at St. Mary's of Aksum, and the manner in which the Italian envoy, Major Ciccodicola, sought to gain influence in Ethiopia, as well as additional facts about the signing of the Americo-Ethiopian treaty itself.

The text which follows is thus a valuable complement to Skinner's published account of the mission, an analysis of which, by Professor Harold G. Marcus, appears in *Ethiopia Observer*, Volume VII, No. 2.

CHAPTER III

of Robert Skinner's unpublished manuscript "Recollections of Life in the Foreign Service of the United States."

There was much speculation, in 1903, as to the purpose of the President in sending a mission to Ethiopia. Our fellow citizens, then only vaguely conscious of the existence of Ethiopia, were surprised to read a London announcement that " big ideas lurked behind the trip," and could not imagine what those " big ideas " were. The only really satisfactory report on Ethiopia they found was contained in the tenth chapter of the Firs[t] Book of Kings which indicated that it was running i[n] King Solomon's mind to occupy the country, exactly a[s] the Italians had expected to do in 1896, when the[y] suffered their humiliating defeat at Adowa. The Quee[n] of Sheba, no doubt alarmed by the rumors which cam[e] to her of Solomon's intentions, decided to go down t[o] Jerusalem herself, armed with her mother's wit, he[r] beauty and perhaps better still " very much gold an[d] precious stones" to find out. The immediate results o[f] her inquiry were so disturbing that " there was no mor[e] spirit in her." She said to the King: " It was a tru[e] report that I heard in mine own land of thy acts an[d] of thy wisdom." She had already " communed wit[h] him of all that was within her heart " and, anticipatin[g] somewhat upon the arts and wiles of Cleopatra sh[e] resolved to see what a present would do. "And she gav[e] the King a hundred and twenty talents of gold, and o[f] spices very great store and precious stones; there cam[e] no more such abundance of spices as these which th[e] Queen of Sheba gave to King Solomon." Solomon wa[s] charmed. Apparently he abandoned his imperialisti[c] designs on Ethiopia " And King Solomon gave th[e] Queen of Sheba all her desire, whatsoever she asked so she turned and went to her country, she and he[r] servants."

The Ethiopian tradition, I discovered, completed th[e] story in the First Book of Kings most satisfactoril[y]. The Queen of Sheba's sojourn in Jerusalem had bee[n] protracted, she saw a good deal of Solomon, and befor[e] her return to her own country, she gave birth to th[e] infant Menelik I, who remained behind in his father['s] care, until he attained to man's estate when he, too, se[t] out for Ethiopia, with King Solomon's blessing and [a] gift of inestimable value: The Tables of Law. It was th[e] intention of his father, King Solomon, that these Table[s] should be a replica of the original Tables in the Ark o[f] the Covenant, but owing to some error, the replica an[d] the original were confused and the young Meneli[k] departed with the original stone which was deposite[d] in the holy city of Axum. Thus was founded the imperi[al] line of Ethiopia from which is directly descended th[e] present Emperor Haile Sellassie.

Against this background of biblical history, poetr[y] and tradition the ends sought by our American missio[n] seemed commonplace indeed. Probably Theodo[re] Roosevelt was not unwilling, at the particular time, t[o] have the American Flag carried conspicuously to Add[is] Ababa, the seat of the one remaining government i[n] East Africa, upon whose vast territories the gre[at]

31

European powers and especially Italy, looked hungrily; and as for the Emperor Menelik II, " the Lion of the Tribe of Juda, chosen of the Lord, King of Kings of Ethiopia," he, certainly, was happy to welcome the representative of a power unsuspected of any territorial designs. It was not a bad idea that the European powers should know that he had friends elsewhere. However, the official and avowed objects of the mission were, as I have mentioned, commonplace. The population of Ethiopia required immense quantities of cotton sheetings for their usual garments, and we were then enjoying a practical monopoly of this important business. We had never taken the pains to protect our situation by establishing normal relations with the government of the Negus, as the Emperor was called, and we needed a commercial treaty with him wich would prevent us, in the event of political complications, from being placed at a disadvantage as respects the European powers. These were the " big ideas " which might have disturbed London less had London known more about them, and which led to my appointment as the head of our first mission to Ethiopia and to my presence in Washington that summer to talk things over with the President and the Acting Secretary of State, Francis B. Loomis.

The heat of Washington in midsummer was almost insupportable but the old Shoreham, with its marble floors and white clad negro servants, seemed relatively cool. The buttermilk fed was then passing over the country, and in the basement bar of the Shoreham could be seen at any moment, a row of men, all drinking the famous Walker-Gordon buttermilk. Mr. Loomis, much interested in the mission, had done everything possible to make it a success. I was to sail for the port of Djibouti in one of Admiral Cotton's ships then lying at Naples, I was to be escorted from the coast to Addis Ababa by a naval guard of thirty men, and to be relieved of as many material cares as possible. The President was taking a personal interest in the mission and seemed sorry he could not go along himself. When the various details had been worked out I went to him at eight o'clock one morning to take leave. Though Washington was at its hottest, he strode up and down his office, looking as fresh as the rose in his buttonhole immaculate in a thin grey frock coat, and tossing off a new subject with each turn of his ceaseless march. The whole thing would be simply splendid – no, the Ethiopians were not negroes but of Semitic stock – there would be lions and elephants, too – a primitive society such as that, must be much like society in the time of Christ – look into the old Christian culture – the monophysite doctrine, a terribly complicated matter – we must think of the United States and they had plants in their parched regions which might well be tried out here – and don't forget those Grevy zebras; they say they can go three or four days without water, huge beasts, too – we must try to cross breed those zebras to get a new kind of mule for our South-western deserts. It was an electrifying conversation, the sort of conversation to convince the Commissioner (I was to be entitled " Commissioner and Plenipotentiary ") that his mission was just about the most important undertaking of the Roosevelt administration.

Several weeks later, on an October morning, I stepped ashore at Djbouti, the capital of French Somaliland and, escorted by my imposing staff, traversed the Place Menelik, en route to Government House to pay our respects to the Governor. The heat shimmered up from the hot earth, no human being was visible anywhere, and as we crossed the Place Menelik a monstrous yawning leopard rose from his disturbed slumber and looked hard at us. We, also, were disturbed by the apparition, but the leopard resumed his rest. As we had to return that way, we were relieved when the Governor told us that the creature was not quite a leopard, but a cheetah, of the same family, sometimes known as the hunting leopard of India.

We had come to Djbouti in the ancient gun boat *Machias* with as fine a group of passengers on board as had ever been assembled for a diplomatic mission. My civilian staff was limited to a secretary, Horatio Wales and a physician, Dr. PerLee Pease, and my faithful coloured servant Hubert Riviere. The military escort consisted of thirty stalwart United States Marines under the command of the then Major and later Colonel George Thorpe. We had been preceded to Djbouti by Lieutenant and later Admiral Charles Lincoln Hussey, who was charged with the preparation of local arrangements. We formed a happy family, lived together in the most intimate manner possible, and we separated eventually with sincere regrets. I shall not attempt to go into the picturesqueness and variety of our journey across country, a journey now made in a day or two, but at that time requiring (in our case) twenty-two days. We travelled by rail across French Somaliland to Dire Douah which is on the Ethiopian frontier, where Admiral Hussey had organised our caravan consisting of camels with their Arab drivers for our considerable supplies, and mules for officers and escort. What a pity it is that what is called " progress " has now substituted the locomotive for the camel and the mule, for it has destroyed without compensating advantages a wonderful and mysterious world, where simple and inoffensive people, whose only constitution was the Ten Commandments, who believed in the Scriptures as a literal revelation no less than the late William J. Bryan and who practised a life which, in its essentials, was not much different, as Mr. Roosevelt had remarked, from social life in the time of Christ.

The camels set our pace and our encampments were determined by the rare desert watering places. We rose, always, well before dawn, reached the next watering place, usually early in the afternoon and when conditions were favourable, indulged in the luxury of a bath. The bath was made possible by means of an empty Standard Oil tin the bottom of which were punched a number of holes, whereupon the tin was suspended from a tree, and half a dozen Somali attendants forming an energetic water brigade, then kept the tin full until the beneficiary beneath cried " enough." Oh! for the luxury of an Ethiopian bath after a day's journey, and the charm of an evening on the desert afterwards! At this hour as the sun began to sink, we might expect to see a troop of polite villagers approaching, bringing with them fowls, eggs, sheep, milk carried in jars on the heads of comely maidens, vegetables, barley for the mules, and a delectable beverage called " tedj " also in large earthen jars. With grave courtesy the visitors would form a semicircle around my chair, offer their gifts, accept money in return and go their way. Occasionally they would organise what was called a " fantasia," a native dance

32

of solemn description which continued until the participants were exhausted. Occasionally torrential rains soaked everything and made tent life miserable, but we always managed to start a fire and to organise some sort of a meal, followed by a generous distribution of quinine pills by our doctor. The Marines had their mess and our smaller officer's mess was ministered to by a remarkable Arab cook who would set off in the morning on foot with a few cooking utensils hung about his neck; on arrival at destination he would find three round stones, start a fire between them and serve an excellent and substantial repast, on time, without a murmur and as a part of the ordinary day's work.

Before crossing the desert we paid a visit to the important commercial city of Harrar to see the Ras Makonnen, a great privincial governor, and the father of Haile Sellassie, then a child playing around the palace when we called. The Ras Makonnen like all well-born Ethiopians (he was the Emperor's nephew) had exquisite manners and was extremely good looking. He possessed regular and delicate features, had small hands and feet, and in his white garments, with a red bordered " chamma " of fine hand woven cotton floating like a Roman toga from his shoulders, made a very striking figure. On his first visit to our camp one hot afternoon, after the ritualistic exchanges of courtesy, his first inquiry was why we kept one of our Marines pacing up and down in front of a certain tent. It was explained that our stock of silver Maria Theresa thalers was stored in the tent. He said mildly: " Better send him away. He is not used to our sun and he will fall ill. Besides, nothing will be stolen." – And nothing was stolen though the guard was dispensed with immediately. Not only was nothing stolen, but even those things of which we desired to unburden ourselves – a used toothbrush for example – were sure to be picked up and restored to the places where they were supposed to belong. When the Ras Makonnen observed that among our many camp stools there was not one chair with a back he said to me: " You will need a chair with a back . . . Such chairs are very restful after a day in the saddle, and I never travel without one. I shall send you one of my own." This he did to the comfort of its every occupant.

Our route after leaving Harrar, took us through the Danakil country inhabited by dangerous savage tribes.

They met us in considerable numbers at our camping places and would sit for hours, on their haunches, like curious children, staring at us, constantly brushing their white sharp pointed teeth with the end of a twig. These Danakils lived a completely nomadic existence, possessed no property other than a few sheep or goats, but maintained certain rigid social distinctions among themselves. Although without any written records or language anyone of these savages could recite his own genealogy for five hundred years, and a Frenchman of my acquaintance, by means of oral testimony of this kind, had succeeded in piecing together quite a complete and instructive tribal history of the race. We were not in the least disturbed by our desert friends, who could obtain firearms only clandestinely, and were armed with nothing more serious than long knives and spears. They had learned to be most respectful of the authority of the Emperor Menelik, who permitted no trifling with the desert caravans. However, we did have one midnight camp alarm, when the sentries reported the presence of many threatening figures on the crest of an eminence whence they could look down upon our tents. In the brilliant moonlight they could be plainly seen and their voices heard. All the guards were called out and under Major Thorpe half of them set out to reconnoitre back of the hill. Half an hour later Major Thorpe returned, convulsed with laughter, to report that what he had taken to be human figures were only large monkeys eager to find out what was going on, and who scampered away when the soldiers drew near.

We reached the higher and richer lands of the real Ethiopia, after travelling about ten days across the desert and after another week of travel came into contact with the first representatives of the government come to tell us of the reception arrangements. We had anticipated a friendly reception at the entrance to the capital with, perhaps, a small escort of honour to lead the way, but were astounded to find, not a guard of honour awaiting us, but what appeared to be an entire army. Literally there were thousands of them, some guessed five and some more, foot soldiers and cavalrymen, with a band of music equipped with monstrous brass horns, which Thorpe vowed were ancient shawms, to add to the excitement. As we neared them the cavalry, mounted on small fiery and gaily caparisoned horses, dashed about in circles emitting loud cries and firing off their rifles while at the same time a salute was fired from the cannon captured from the Italians several years before. Officers and men wore loose fitting white cotton tunics and trousers, red bordered " chammas " and over the " chammas " mantles of lion and leopard skins. Every man in addition to his rifle carried also a spear and a decorated buckler. The half barbaric scene, in the clear sunlight of the Ethiopian plateau, was bewilderingly beautiful.

Our own officers and men, not wishing to be outdone, made the bravest possible showing. Hussey and Thorpe were magnificent under their plumed chapeaus and our Marines were superb in bearing and costume, but it happened that the sartorial honours went most unexpectedly to the three civilian members of the mission who, mounted on mules, wore black dress suits and shiny top hats. Now the populace of Addis Ababa, who lined our pathway and shouted their welcome, had seen many arriving missions before. The Europeans always came weighted down with gold braid, sashes and jewelled decorations – but there was something new, unheard of, pontifical, a swallow tail coat and a stove pipe hat! Several months later when our mission finally broke up and we made presents to our excellent retainers of useless equipment, my own tent boy, who wore his shirt outside of his trousers and invariably carried strapped to his side a scimitar (useful for defence or for cutting grass for the mules), humbly begged that he might receive as a special mark of benevolence, my battered top hat. His name was " Slave of the Holy Ghost." He departed from my sight the envy of all his fellows, now wearing the official top hat.

We were eventually organised into a decorous procession and conducted to the vast hall where the Emperor Menelik, seated upon his carpeted throne, under a silken canopy, awaited us surrounded by his court dignitaries. The scene was one of dignity and the ceremony quickly over. After the speeches the Emperor, a friendly man of lively wit, asked many questions through the

33

court interpreter, hoped we should enjoy ourselves in his country, and said that he had assigned a palace for our occupancy as long as we remained. The palace proved to be an enormous empty, thatched, barn-like building the ample grounds of which were surrounded by a palisade so that we had plenty of space for the erection of our tents and were protected from curious eyes by the palisade. We were scarcely settled in our temporary home before an abundant "hospitality" consisting of food for man and beast in great variety and quantity arrived with the Emperor's compliments. A day or two later he came in person with his entire court to pay us a visit, a high officer holding an immense red umbrella over his head when he arrived and when he departed.

The Emperor invited us to dine with him the following Sunday, together with all our newly made friends of the diplomatic corps. At this dinner we found ourselves on an elevated platform not unlike the stage of a theatre, in the same large hall in which we had been received, with a curtain separating our platform from the body of the hall. On the platform sat the Emperor under a dais supported by gold columns, from which he greeted his guests affably as they passed to a long table laid in the European style. The Emperor was served apart with native dishes only, but an empty chair at our table was supposed to indicate symbolically his presence with us. Silent white robed vassals served the conventional meal prepared for us, which was supplemented by a number of the choicest native dishes passed over from the Emperor's throne for the satisfaction of our curiosity. They were mostly preparations of beef and red pepper of such fiery quality that curiosity was easily satisfied. For the consumption of these dishes there had been placed before each guest a stack of thin meal cakes resembling so many griddle cakes, and on this stack of "ingeras" the food was placed, to be eaten with the fingers, bread and all, thus leaving a fresh "inger" for the next course. Meanwhile the servants plied us with French wine, first reassuring us by pouring a few drops in their own hands and swallowing them. When at last the dinner came to an end, the Emperor dipped his fingers into a silver basin and then passed it on to us, after which the curtains were drawn so we might see the thousand or more subjects who had assembled in the body of the hall, seated on the floor, waiting to feast on the Emperor's bounty. We remained several hours watching the curious spectacle and observing the Emperor carrying on innumerable consultations with his people, the occasion being one which seemed to serve as a substitute for our democratic processes, as it enabled the public to see their ruler face to face and to submit to him such petitions or complaints as they wished.

After the Emperor's dinner came a round of less official dinner parties at our own and at all the legations. Although the members of the diplomatic corps, eyed each other politically with unremitting suspicion, they were nevertheless reduced to each other's society for relaxation, and as far as the amenities went, got along very well together. Happily material life was cheap, because an innocent dinner party for ten people involved the provision of food for at least three hundred, as every chief of mission went forth with his armed guard of thirty men who expected entertainment no less than their masters. There was, perhaps, no more need to be accompanied by an armed guard of these proportions than in the city of Washington, but it seemed to be required as a face saving operation and did no harm.

The diplomatic negotiations over our treaty went on smoothly, but they demanded time, and in the interval the history and institutions of the country gave us plenty to think and talk about. One of the best sources of information on these matters was M. Chefneux, the Emperor's French counsellor. When I asked him what substance of truth underlay the Ethiopian tradition that the actual Mosaic Tables of the Law had been brought from Jerusalem by the first Menelik in the time of King Solomon, he replied that no Ethiopian ecclesiastic questioned the tale and that the precious stone was under constant guard in the holy city of Axum. He permitted me to copy a letter on this subject, from his own correspondent at Axum, the English translation of which is as follows:

> "I am writing you from Axum about the Mosaic tablets, which are here. All Ethiopians, especially those in this region, are firm in their conviction that the original stone is here. No one is permitted to approach the place where it is guarded. It lies in a small room at the side of the Axum church within the sacred enclosure. I have said no one is permitted to approach this place, but exception is made of a single priest who enters during the various solemnities to offer incense, but when he does he turns his face away. According to tradition, no one, without committing a sacriligious act, may even fix his regard upon the place where the tablet reposes. Such being the usage and the tradition, it follows that no one can be found who has seen the stone and who is capable of supplying details. It is said that in the time of Dedjaz Oubia who ruled between 1830 and 1850, a group of Armenians accompanying one of their great bishops came to Axum especially to see this stone. After serious discussion with the Ethiopians they were permitted to view it – in any case their bishop was allowed to do so and it is affirmed here that he gave assurance that the stone was truly the Tablet of Sion."

True or false, it is certainly profoundly interesting to know that during long centuries, long before the dawn of the Christian era, a stone has lain in the church of Axum which the faithful believe to be the actual Tables of Law received by Moses on Mount Sinai and afterwards deposited in the Temple at Jerusalem. What has happened at Axum since 1904 when I copied the above letter I do not know. It is to be hoped that the Italians during their brief occupation of the country respected this ancient relic.

The story of the Tables of Law gains in interest when we recall that they are the background of all Ethiopian jurisprudence. Until Christianity was introduced in the fourth century, Ethiopia got along comfortably enough with only the Ten Commandments, but when Christianity was introduced the Coptic church became the church of Ethiopia, and a written law of the church was also accepted, a code known as the Fetha Nagast composed it is said, of texts from the Old and New Testaments and apocryphal apostolic writings. I visited with the Abouna, the venerable and learned head of the Ethiopian church, who had been appointed to his office by the Coptic authorities in Alexandria, and who seemed to think that the holy texts which constitute the Ethiopian law worked about as well as our more elaborate legislation, and were quite as applicable to every conceivable circumstance in modern life. Certainly the fathers of the church appeared to have found and dealt with problems which we vainly think belong only to our own times, as for example a law of corporations requiring that the capital be determined and the division of the profits specified; a law prohibiting dealings in future corps; and a law of fiduciary responsibility.

When I talked with M. Chefneux about the institution of slavery he told me that in a primitive civilisation such as that of Ethiopia a land without industries, in which practically all trades were carried on by barter, a sort of feudal system had been evolved, not really slavery, but the only kind of system that would work. At the top of the system stood the Emperor, below him the provincial governors, and below them the local chiefs whose vassals might be called slaves if one wished to do so, but whose relationship to the chiefs was defined and satisfactory. To their chiefs they gave loyalty, fought for them when need be against the savages in the desert, and in return they received from their chiefs land for their own cultivation and a guaranteed subsistence. Bruce, the first Englishman to visit Ethiopia two centuries ago, seems to have shared this same feeling about slavery as M. Chefneux. Bruce relates with much humour the experience of a parish priest of his acquaintance who had a large family to support and scarcely any income. The priest decided to ease the situation by sending his eldest son to a friendly chieftain to become the latter's slave. The son was so happy in the new environment that the second son now insisted that he, too, be sent into slavery. Thereupon the priest gave us his second son, but only to find that his eldest daughter next complained bitterly of parental partiality and neglect, so she, likewise, had to be sent into slavery after which the family lived in peace.

We were not long in discovering that although Italy had been defeated at Adowa several years earlier, Italian designs upon the country remained unchanged and that the little Italian minister, Major Ciccodicola, with patience and infinite pains, was endeavouring to restore the prestige of his country by the old fashioned processes of bribery and corruption. He was presently vexed because sometime before our arrival the Emperor had given out that he intended to remove the capital from Addis Ababa to Addis Alem whereupon the Italian government had caused a very fine stone legation building to be erected in the new capital site; but no sooner had the legation been completed than the Emperor announced urbanely that he thought he would not change the capital after all!

Major Ciccodicola was a companionable person, fond of talking and on the occasion of my first call, after I had complimented him upon his grasp of the local situation he answered that his task had been made easy by his " system." When asked what his " system " was he said: " I will show you." He then produced a large box filled with small watches. " The Ethiopians," said he, " like nothing so much as a watch. When I want to know something I find the right man and I give him a watch. Thus I have my eyes and ears everywhere."

We soon ascertained how the busy little Major's system worked in practice. In the atmosphere of intrigue in which he lived it was doubtless impossible for him to abstain from inquiry into the course of our diplomatic negotiations. Possibly it passed through his mind that our proposed treaty contained some secret clause that might run counter to the great Italian project of swallowing up the entire empire. In any event, work on the treaty went forward quietly and the day was at hand when we might expect to sign it and start back to the coast. Now in Ethiopia writing paper is something rare, and governments insist that formal treaties be written on a special and expensive sort of paper, each sheet of which is divided into two columns so that the usual two languages of the text may appear side by side. I had brought with me a provision of such paper and had sent some to the Ethiopian scribes on which to make the necessary treaty copies. I happened to be paying a call on my Italian colleague the day before the one fixed for signing the fair copies, and mentioned to him that we were to sign next day and afterwards to leave almost at once. Thereupon Major Ciccodicola, out of the fullness of his knowledge, remarked: " No, you are not signing tomorrow. You must remain with us much longer than you suppose."

" But we are signing tomorrow," I insisted, " and then we are leaving Addis Ababa."

" I am sorry," he persisted, " but you are mistaken. The scribes have upset the contents of an ink bottle on the prepared copies and they have no more treaty paper. You will have to wait."

The Major should have kept the secret to himself. He was right about the ink, perhaps it was he who had suggested the " spilling "; but he did not know that there was plenty of treaty paper in reserve, and thanks to his telling me in time I was able to have fresh copies made with a trusted observer on hand to see that no more ink was spilled. Thus the treaty was signed and sealed according to programme and for more than thirty years it regulated our relations with Ethiopia in fairly satisfactory manner.

Our quest for garden seeds for dry regions and for Grevy zebras for breeding purposes met with no diplomatic opposition! Neither the British, French or Italian legations cared in the least about garden seeds or a new kind of mule. It really required more than a year before the zebras were found, two beautiful creatures one-third taller than the more common species, and they reached the United States safely. Unfortunately one died and the other broke his neck in Washington by plunging violently against a stone wall so the new mule for Arizona and New Mexico that could travel four days without water never was bred, and soon the advent of the motor truck deprived the project of its interest.

At last our work had been accomplished, we could pay our farewell visits and return to the *Machias* awaiting us at Djbouti. We were ready now for our last audience of the Emperor of whose thoughtful kindness we were to have a new manifestation. We were all present at the audience, officers and the entire Marine guard. Two members of the original guard were absent, having been taken ill before our departure from the coast and they remained, therefore, on ship board. The Emperor chatted in his usual animated way and then directed his aide-de-camp to distribute some simple silver medals to each of the guards. When the distribution was over two medals remained on the tray, and these he asked me to give to the two sick men at Djbouti. " I would like

35

them to know," said he, " that they have not been forgotten." In the course of the same audience the Emperor asked if I liked his " tedj." He was assured that I did – it is a most refreshing beverage of fermented honey. He did not recur to the subject but as we progressed homeward, every evening at sunset, a messenger invariably arrived at my tent bearing on his or her head, a large earthen jar of the Emperor's " tedj." He had not forgotten! We left the palace charged with decorations, also with the traditional gifts to diplomatic visitors consisting of a beautifully worked buckler studden with gold nails, a sword of honour and two spears, and for the President a magnificent elephant's tusk and two lion cubs. It is not easy to travel with two vigorous lion cubs, but we somehow managed it, only one, however, surviving the journey. Our long procession moved quietly out of Addis Ababa, camels and innumerable little asses going ahead, we following, accompanied for several miles according to the custom of the country, by the friends we had made, and the long journey to the terminus of the railroad at Dire Douah began.

Some weeks later we were again at Djbouti, happy that our mission had been successfully accomplished, and regretting that we must now separate after an association that had been so happy in every way. Before the final dispersion of our group, my Ethiopian interpreter, Waldo Georgis, a young man of refined features and black as coal, came to me and removing from his neck an antique Greek cross of beautifully worked filigree silver, asked that he be permitted to give it to me. " My mother gave me this cross," said he, " I have always worn it, and should be pleased if you would wear it now. We shall never meet again, but your God is my God, and I am sure that my mother would wish you to have it." With this final touch of sentiment and ceremony the mission came to an end.

36

Yohannes IV and Menelik II

European imperialism in Africa was still rampant at this time, but Menelik's victory at Adowa kept him pretty much free of this pressure for at least ten years. However, there were problems with regional leaders, the lords, princes, and kings, but it was with such matters that Menelik showed his diplomatic skill. By Ethiopian tradition only the emperor could create a king, but Menelik chose not to appoint any kings. To do so was usually a sign of weakness. Also by Ethiopian tradition, a prince could only be appointed by an emperor or a king. Menelik did appoint many princes. At the same time he chose to ignore the claims of some families who had previously by tradition, or heredity, held the position. In this manner Menelik was assured of the loyalty of those he had appointed.

In addition, Menelik was very skillful in the use of marriages to strengthen his control of Ethiopia. For example, his fourth wife was the formidable Empress Taitu who was of Galla origin, a tribe that always seemed to be opposing Ethiopian emperors. One of his cousins was married to an important man in the Lasta province. Another cousin was a king who controlled Harar and the Ogaden. One of his daughters was married to the prince of another province. And as Hess the historian said, *"and so it went."*

Menelik adopted a new device to replace the disloyal regional leaders and to strengthen those who were loyal – the beginnings of a centralized ministerial government. This was, to the best of my knowledge, the first attempt of any emperor to establish such a system. At first the system looked good, but as Hess noted it was dependant on one man, Menelik. Unfortunately, about this time his health began to fail, with several strokes occurring. It became impossible for him to oversee and make the decisions required. When this happened, court intrigues, attempted coups, and rivalries among influential families for political power took place. The struggle to see who would be the successor to the throne was getting underway.

Menelik II had begun to establish the foundation for a central government and had learned that in a government the size required to run Ethiopia, delegation of authority was necessary. High ranking ministers (cabinet officers) were needed, but there was no mention of a constitution that would detail and establish rules of government on a continuing basis. It is likely that had Menelik remained in good health, he would have seen the necessity for the addition of these institutional factors. Certainly he was viewed by most Ethiopians as a legend. After all, he had established a new capital, Addis Ababa, and defeated the Italians at the battle of Adowa. Also of great importance, he had moved Ethiopia further in the direction of becoming a modern African country.

A Successor to Menelik II

Menelik II died around the end of 1913. The struggle to see who would take his place had begun earlier. His wife the empress had tried to do what she could, but was limited until a successor had been decided upon. In 1908 the emperor's grandson, Lij Iasu, had been designated as his successor. This proved to be disastrous when a few years later he began favoring the Muslims. Also the European imperialist were still actively pursuing a protectorate over Ethiopia and Lij Iasu seemed to be interested in a deal. At this point Lij Iasu publicly announced he had converted to the Islamic faith. This was too much for the Ethiopians and they overthrew him in 1916. According to Hess, the leaders of the coup "included Ras Wolde Gorgis, Ras Kassa Hailuof Gojjam, the Abuna Mattewos, various Shoan nobles, Ras Tafari Makonen, son of Menelik's cousin Makonen, and Menelik's Minister of War, Habte Giorgis. The nobility, the church, and the army joined to overthrow Lij Iasu.

The coup was successful, but a program for Ethiopia was difficult to decide. It was finally agreed that Menelik's daughter Zawditu would reign as empress but she would not rule. A regent was elected by the nobles to rule. They agreed upon Ras Tafari, a distant cousin of Menelik II. Hess speculates that the nobles likely thought they could have their way with Ras Tafari, malleable was the term used by Hess to describe why he was given the position.

Ras Tafari Makonen

Ethiopia was being ruled as a triumvirate after the overthrow of Lij Iasu. Due to powerful support from the nobility, Habte Giorgis, a highly respected general was in charge of the military. Queen Zawditu, the empress, had loyalty but little power. Events soon proved that the real power was with Ras Tafari who had been appointed regent. The general died in 1926, as did the Abuna (head of church). The Abuna was not a part of the triumvirate, but the religious factor was always important in the decision making process in Ethiopia. Ras Tafari was regent from 1916 to 1930 when he became the Negus (emperor). During that 14 years he accumulated considerable experience and power. He successfully put down uprisings, and thwarted an alleged attempt by Queen Zawditu and a conservative noble, Dejazmatch Balcha, to overthrow him. The queen later obeyed the wishes of Ras Tafari and nominated him heir to the throne. Zawditu's former husband, Ras Gugsa Wolie, made one final attempt to overthrow him but failed. Subsequently, the empress died and Ras Tafari Makonen became emperor of Ethiopia in 1930. He selected Haile Selassie as his throne name.

Rastafarianism

I expect not many people know there is a link between Ras Tafari and Rastafarianism. This is a religion that began in Jamaica, and believes that Ras Tafari (Haile Selassie) is the living god of this religion. This religion is what I chose to describe as freewheeling. Among other ideas it praises the spiritual effects of marijuana, and believes in superiority of the black race. Its music and teachings are laden with elements of spiritualism and mysticism. Bob Marley, a Jamaican singer, guitarist, song writer, and pioneer of Jamaican reggae, is a disciple of the Rastafarian movement. His music has been a significant contributor to the movement. I feel sure Haile Selassie's designation as the God of Rastafarianism religion was not of his making, but I do believe he was made aware of his role as it's God.*

**Information provided by Encarta 2002 – key word Rastafarianism.*

Emperor Haile Selassie (1930-1974)

As regent, Selassie had begun to implement plans to modernize Ethiopia. A number of these plans had been started by Emperor Tewodros and Menelik II. For example, they had seen the need to centralize the military and take control from province leaders. They had realized that the military should no longer rob the peasants for their pay and food. The military should be trained and professional. The provinces should be united to form an effective central government that would strengthen the country to the benefit of all sectors. It needed to build an industrial sector and produce more goods for import. Prior to Selassie, Tewodros and Menelik had tried to carry out most of these objectives, but had failed. As noted, their failure was largely due to opposition by the deeply entrenched nobility and church. Selassie was aware of the attempts of the two previous emperors and something of the reasons for their failure. Based on my study of the history of Ethiopia, I have come to the conclusion that the two previous emperors were well meaning and wanted to modernize and improve living conditions – social and economic – in Ethiopia. Both had strong egos and enjoyed the power of ruling and achieving. The desire for personal wealth did not drive them. Haile Selassie had some of the same traits as these two – ego and the enjoyment of ruling, but his ideas for modernizing Ethiopia were broader and more advanced.

For example, early in his reign (1931) he developed a constitution that contained most of the essential language and clauses found in the constitutions of the highly developed Western countries. Actually, this document was necessary in order to convince the developed countries to aid Ethiopia. A careful reading of a later version (1955) would reveal language that put the emperor in complete control of the actions called for in the constitution. He had veto power over any actions taken by members of the bicameral parliament called for in the constitution. Not only that, but he could affect the election of who might serve in the parliament. Hess states: *"The Constitution of 1955 establishes a constitutional monarchy, but not a Western style constitution"*. Article 26, for example states *"the sovereignty of the empire is vested in the emperor and the supreme authority over all affairs of the empire is exercised by him as head of the state."* Hess refers to this as: constitutionalized absolutism. Students who had studied abroad and were now serving in the parliament recognized this aspect for what it was, and many resented it. Some were now bold enough to express their displeasure.

Before getting into Sellassie's ideas and programs for modernizing Ethiopia, let us look at his education. He was educated in Ethiopia by French Jesuits and this seemed to influence him to prefer French culture and institutions. He spoke French fluently. He visited the French military academy and sent Ethiopians there to become officers in the Ethiopian army. One has to remember that the level of education in Ethiopia at the time Haile Selassie was being schooled was very low. In fact, most of the schools were religious, and while Selassie did not reach a high grade level his education was more comprehensive and superior to that of the church schools. Haile Selassie was highly intelligent and a diligent scholar. In my readings I came across a statement that he only had a fourth grade education. I disagree.

In early 1936 Fascist Italy decided to attempt a takeover of Ethiopia. Having a superior military force equipped with airplanes, poison gas, and tanks, it took only a short time to overrun the country. Haile Selassie was forced to flee to England. There he delivered an eloquent impassioned speech to the United Nations Assembly noting that Ethiopia was a member of the United Nations and as such was entitled to support from them. It was a famous speech. Selassie was correct when he said Ethiopia was entitled to support from the United Nations, but the body declined his request. Ethiopia was sacrificed. I conclude this action was taken because the United Nation Assembly thought it was necessary to avoid the outbreak of a larger war. The action may have postponed a larger war, but it did not prevent one. It was not many years later that WWII began, a war that may have been encouraged by decisions that were conciliatory to the Germans and Italians.

Back in Ethiopia, as mentioned, it did not take long for the Italians to seize the capital, Addis Ababa, and the major cities such as Gondar, Axum, etc. It is noted that in some places the Italians were aided by Ethiopians who were opposed to Emperor Haile Selassie and his policies. Hess cites one example: Ras (Prince) Hailu of Gojjam thought this a proper time to even the score with Haile Selassie for refusing to appoint him king of Gojjam. Hailu had been ordered to leave Ethiopia at the same time Haile Selassie left for exile in England, but he managed to remain behind and to work out a deal with the Italians that allowed him to become King of Gojjam. There were others, who for one reason or another supported the Italians, but fortunately there was more support by Ethiopian guerrilla patriots. At one point during the five year occupation there was an attempt to assassinate the Italian leader, Graziani. This released a reign of terror and for weeks thereafter hundreds of Ethiopians were massacred. Primarily in danger were those who had been educated abroad, and those who had supported the efforts of Haile Selassie to modernize Ethiopia. Wisely, the Italians appointed a new administrator to replace Graziani, the Duke of Aosta. Although conditions calmed down, it was not enough to make it safe for Italians in the countryside. Addis Ababa was described as a heavily fortified military garrison during the entire five year occupation.

Italy had visions of Ethiopia becoming a granary, a provider of other supplies and raw materials. Italy expected that Italians would become settlers. It poured money into the development of Ethiopia, particularly into building roads and bridges. Italy also invested in modernizing some of the cities, not to mention the cost of invading and maintaining a military force in Ethiopia. Italian soldiers were killed. It was not long before the Italians realized the gains did not equal the losses. For example, the countryside was not pacified. Consequently, little in the way of produce was coming in. It was impossible to collect any revenues from the peasants, always a difficult task no matter who was running the country. Not even the emperor had been able to do this. Foreign capital was not coming in. No petroleum in commercial quantities was discovered.

The Italians did not voluntarily give up and leave. Italy declared war on Britain in June of 1940 and the British feared the Italians in Ethiopia would invade the Sudan. The British decided to move first. They contacted General Sandford, who had served as the British Consul in Ethiopia, and with his help planned a three pronged attack on the Italians in Ethiopia. Skipping some of the details, Ethiopian refugees trained and led by the British entered Gojjam in early march of 1941. By the end of March the Italians had been defeated on all three fronts. The Ethiopians were completely liberated from the Italians, but not from the British.

At this point the British considered Ethiopia as occupied enemy territory, but the Ethiopians would have none of this. They regarded Ethiopia as a liberated country. After a bit of discussion, Britain recognized Ethiopia as a sovereign country but with some limitations. A year later these limitations were eliminated. Whatever lingering thoughts the British may have had about ruling any part of Ethiopia were eliminated when Haile Selassie began to aspire to an international role for Ethiopia. He made numerous trips to the United States, the Soviet Union, India, Japan, Yugoslavia, France, and the Arab states. Ethiopia, since 1950, had taken an active role in the United Nations, particularly at the Disarmament Conference in Geneva, and on the committee that dealt with decolonization. Haile Selassie was looked upon as the major figure in African politics. As mentioned elsewhere, Ethiopia had been occupied for a short while but was never colonized. Haile Selassie had taken the lead role in preventing Italy from accomplishing its ambition of taking over Ethiopia and had driven its occupation force out. Moreover it had persuaded the United Nations to cede control of Eritrea to Ethiopia.

As a side note, when I was in Ethiopia some thirty years later, I had the pleasure of meeting two of General Sandford's sons. By this time the general had been given extensive land holdings in Ethiopia not far from Addis Ababa. Produce from this plantation, especially livestock, was being sold in Addis Ababa. My wife, Agnes, had the good fortune to meet the general's wife at a luncheon in Martha Caldwell's home in Addis.

Following the liberation of Ethiopia Haile Selassie renewed his efforts to modernize the country. He was aided in this effort by the British occupation that made it possible for the administration to give more attention to what was taking place in the provinces. This had always been a major weakness of central government. Administration never had the resources to regularly oversee provincial operations to determine they were following actions agreed upon at the central level.

Haile Selassie continued to send young men abroad to be educated. Unfortunately, many of those trained prior to the occupation were killed trying to liberate Ethiopia or by the Italians who were trying to gain control of Ethiopia. Haile Selassie set up a government sponsored school system that to some extent replaced the church school system. With help from the University of Oklahoma an Agricultural college was established in Harar. In Addis a national library was established in 1944. Also in Addis the University College of Addis Ababa the Haile Selassie I University was established. When I was in Ethiopia (1972-74) a friend of mine, Don Ferguson, was over there on a contract to provide assistance to the University. To the best of my memory, he was the chief advisor in library operations.

It was amazing to me how Haile Selassie could think of the many things that needed to be modernized in Ethiopia and set about to get the job done. For example, the water works system in Addis Ababa was primitive. A water works specialist was brought in to install a new system. This specialist, an American and his wife, lived in the same apartment building we did. We were friends for the two years we lived there and so we had firsthand knowledge of this situation. Our friend informed us that the new plant produced water free of any harmful disease. However, once the water left the plant in old pipe lines that were likely to be corroded and broken in places all kinds of harmful bacteria would contaminate the water supply entering consumption areas. This specialist had all his water boiled and filtered just as we did.

Another area we had direct knowledge of was the income tax system, it was archaic in Ethiopia. The person sent over to see what could be done to install a workable system, was also a friend who lived in our apartment complex. Without going into too many details, a major obstacle was the lack of mailing addresses for potential tax payers. This was true for businesses as well as individuals. People who received mail did so by having it sent to post office boxes. My friend and his colleagues devised a temporary system of showing up with no warning at business places. They would levy a tax based on an on-the-spot appraisal of what the tax should be. I remember when our friend was describing this procedure, I could imagine how these merchants must have been busy concealing merchandise to keep it from the tax collector's sight.

I do know that Haile Selassie tried to collect taxes in the provinces but was met with considerable opposition by peasants and land lords. Hess provides considerable information on tax collecting attempts in Ethiopia. He notes that going back to tax reform legislation in 1942 and 1944 in Gojjam Amhara, there was terrific opposition to this idea and the legislation failed. Again in 1951 and later in 1962 attempts were made to survey peasants, large land lords, and tenant holdings. All resisted and the tax assessors sent provincial army troops in to put down the resistance. Some local tax assessors were shot and the resistance mounted. The central government headed by the emperor decided to back down and the tax plan failed. Other areas in Ethiopia opposed similar plans to collect taxes, and to the best of my knowledge tax collection in the provinces remains a problem.

Haile Selassie, as has been mentioned, was greatly interested in improving education in Ethiopia. He was aware that it was necessary to send students abroad for training. To some extent he was also aware that once these students observed differences in the way countries were governed abroad from those in Ethiopia, they would wonder and begin to question their own system. However, I don't believe he realized the extent they would question and challenge the need for change. In any event, as the number of students sent abroad increased so did their opposition to what they perceived as needs to change the feudal system. It was a system that had existed for over two thousand years in their country, one that had been replaced in Europe for hundreds of years. They looked at countries that had replaced dictatorships with more democratically run governments such as Great Britain with a monarchy that was almost entirely symbolic – a country run by a Parliament and a Prime Minister, that is subject to replacement by the vote of the people. Of course many of these students came to the United States – an even more democratic country. It was not long before these students were organizing protests that often grew violent. Police and the military were called in to quell these protests. Some students were jailed. Some were shot and the university in Addis Ababa was closed several times. According to Hess, there were times when the students considered the United States Embassy in Addis to be contrary to their interest and in sympathy with those of Haile Selassie and picketed the Embassy. On another occasion they picketed the headquarters of the Peace Corp in Addis. These protests by the student's show they have been effective in bringing about changes in Ethiopia. Undoubtedly, they have been an important factor in the coup d'état that took place in 1974, and I expect in the attempted coup d'état of December 1960.

Dynasties

I regret that while I was working in Ethiopia I had little knowledge or appreciation of the dynastic organization of the country. I had a vague amount of information that Ethiopia had operated as a dynasty, but never heard my Ethiopian colleagues discussing any of the particulars. Looking back, I expect this was not a very popular subject to discuss at that time (1972-74). Haile Selassie was waging a power struggle with some of the lords and nobles. I expect my Ethiopian colleagues, many of whom had been educated in USA colleges, were reluctant to discuss the dynastic structure of the country for fear of being accused of being disloyal to Haile Selassie. Also I am aware now that it was in my best interest not to have been caught up in such discussions. As I gathered material for this book, I soon discovered that before the time of Christ Ethiopia operated as a dynasty very similar to the dynasties that existed in Western European countries. This was very interesting as I had been in at least a dozen other African countries and had not encountered another country that was organized on a dynastic basis. Also of interest, Ethiopia still operated as a dynasty until Haile Selassie was overthrown in 1974. Long before this all the European countries had shed their dynasties. Of course change is very slow in Ethiopia and most other African countries. Certainly this failure to shed the shackles imposed by such a system has taken a toll on the development of Ethiopia.

More About Haile Selassie

Haile Selassie was the longest ruler of all the emperors of Ethiopia, and of any other ruler in Africa. Actually, it is difficult for me to recall any other that ruled as long as he did. He began ruling as regent in 1916 and was ousted in a coup in 1974, a total of 58 years. Selassie was blessed with nearly all of the characteristics of an outstanding leader. I use the term nearly all advisedly and will point out later the flaws as I see them. But first the strong points of this brilliant ruler. He was extremely charismatic, a good speaker, and possessed an unbelievable memory. He was aware of what had to be accomplished in order modernize Ethiopia.

By the 1960s, under the leadership of Haile Selassie, Ethiopia had made some progress in its attempt to become a more modern nation. Agriculture was largely a subsistence industry but according to Hess (Pg. 87) had unlike many others subsistence economies, a rate of growth in agricultural production that continued to exceed the population growth. Total agricultural production has shown an impressive gain of almost 30 percent in the 1959-1969 decenniums, while per capita production for that same period shows an increase of 8 percent." The most popular grain crops are grains, teff, barley, and sorghum. Remember, Mussolini wanted to make Ethiopia into the granary capital of Africa. Coffee is by far the most important export crop of Ethiopia and most of it is exported to the US. **Statistical data from Hess, Chap. 4.*

Cotton production, particularly in the lower Awash Valley area of Ethiopia was promoted, most of it on an irrigated basis. A deal with Mitchell Cotts and Company, a British firm, gave it a plantation concession. In return Cotts promised to provide enough cotton to satisfy Ethiopia's entire demand for cotton in a few years. Production did increase from 2000 metric tons to 8000 metric tons from 1959 to 1969, but consumption also made an exceptionally large increase. Ethiopia still imported more than $1million dollars of cotton from the U.S. alone in 1967. Since that time, additional cotton producing firms have been granted concessions. Cotton manufacturing is Ethiopia's largest manufacturing enterprise. Hess reports that about 65 percent of Ethiopia's gross domestic product is accounted for by agriculture. He cites a figure of around 1.3 billion dollars in 1968 with a per capita figure of about $55. **Statistical data from Hess, Chap 4.*

Sugar production was another product in short supply, so Ethiopia gave a concession to a Dutch firm to come in and produce sugar cane. A refinery was also established and soon Ethiopia did not need to import great quantities of sugar. Because of the potential,

More About Haile Selassie

Haile Selassie was able to borrow money from the World Bank, Western and East European countries, Japan and other investor countries. Selassie was careful to spread these investment deals around so as not to become dependent on any one or two countries. Selassie was also planning to have Ethiopians learn from the technical expertise of the foreign firms so that eventually it would not be necessary to depend upon foreigners to provide the expertise to produce for the country.

Haile Selassie was aware that if he wanted to modernize Ethiopia he must include manufacturing in the process. Unfortunately, the cultural makeup of Ethiopia does not favor industries that involve machinery. Emperor Tewodros was made aware of this when he wanted to produce cannons and other weapons. His solution was to bring in foreign technicians, but he did not insist on Ethiopians learning from the foreigners who were brought in. Selassie was also having to rely on considerable foreign technical help. For example, as mentioned, cotton and sugar manufacturing industries were being operated by outsiders, but Selassie was trying to get Ethiopians more involved in the process. I do recall that my wife bought some rugs that had been produced in a plant manned by Ethiopians, especially by very young workers with nimble fingers. Also there were numerous handicraft items produced there. We did notice that often Muslims were more inclined to engage in business enterprises than were ethnic Ethiopians. Armenians were the best jewelers and were engaged in a number of other enterprises involving, food, clothing, and household items.

There were some enterprises that employed labor and the workers were increasingly becoming aware of the need to organize in order to better working conditions and wages. One example was a labor union that represented the laborers who worked on the railroad from Addis Ababa to Djibouti. On September 5, 1962 the Labor Relations Decree was passed making labor unions legal. It was only a short time later that labor unions became popular with the some 200,000 laborers that existed in Ethiopia about that time. There were nearly fifty labor unions formed. Some were becoming demanding and conducting strikes. One strike occurred in Addis Ababa when an 800 member government printing press union struck for better working conditions and shut down nine newspapers. There was also a bus strike in Addis about this time. These were attention getters, and laborers began to realize the power and value of organizing. At the same time Haile Selassie was becoming aware of the potential danger of this movement to his dictatorial rule. It so happened that Dr. Robert Caldwell was appointed Labor Attaché shortly after my wife and I arrived in Addis. We soon became close friends of the Caldwells, and Robert and I would discuss some of the problems associated with the formation and operations of labor unions in third world countries. Bob was not only the Labor Attaché in Ethiopia but also for several other surrounding countries. As I recall none of these countries were run on a democratic basis, and labor unions were not the most welcome institutions in those countries. Ethiopia was beginning to be significantly influenced by students who had been educated abroad giving them a more democratic outlook on the operations of such institutions as labor unions.

I know that Bob Caldwell fully supported the idea of labor unions and did all he could to help them organize and operate. I also know that his task was difficult and that he was aware of Haile Selassie's aversion to these unions because he considered them a threat to his rule. Selassie was right. These unions, along with numerous other institutions, were opposed to his rule and from time to time challenged the emperor.

Cooperatives, another business institution similar to labor unions, did not seem to be developed to the extent the labor unions were. I base my conclusion on the fact that on a few occasions I was asked to represent the Ministry of Agriculture in meetings with other government institutions on the subject of cooperatives. There did not seem to be much enthusiasm or development of these organizations. If my memory is correct, cooperatives were handled by the ministry responsible for labor unions. I am positive that cooperatives were not serviced by the Ministry of Agriculture. I expect cooperatives were not encouraged by Haile Selassie due to his distaste for any institutions of a democratic nature. Also the dynastic organization of the rural population was inimically opposed to the democratic nature of cooperatives.

Selassie had also managed to get several countries to provide technical assistance to several areas of government administration. Some that I recall were Ministries' of Agriculture and Finance, Military Department, Addis Ababa Water Department, Labor Department, and Education. At this time the United States had a director and a sizeable staff of the U.S. Aid for International Development (USAID) organization in Addis Ababa. The director was responsible for procuring technical personnel to assist the above named agencies. This assistance was provided based on a request from the Ethiopian administration to USAID. After study of the request and a determination that it was needed, a project was developed to provide the aid. In those cases where technicians were provided, the project often called for the Ethiopian Government to pay a portion of the technician's salary. During the two years that I worked in Ethiopia I was paid in small part by the government. It was never explained to me why this was done. My assumption is that the Ethiopian Government believed this arrangement gave them more control over my work.

I also recall some of the other countries involved in providing development assistance operated as described above, especially in agriculture (85% of the country's output). These countries included Great Britain, France, Germany, and Sweden. Also there was at least one Communist country, Bulgaria, that I recall and there may have been others at this time (1972-1974). I attended meetings with advisors from these countries. Ethiopians who represented various government sectors were also present. The meetings that I attended for the most part, were related to the agricultural sector. We were offering advice and coordinating our efforts to improve agricultural production, distribution and marketing. I must say that I did not become aware that conditions in the country were so unstable and getting worse every day until about the middle of 1973. It was then when I began to learn about the drought conditions in some areas of the country. It was at this time a German magazine article came out letting the world know about conditions in Ethiopia. I am sure the Ethiopian press as well as many Ethiopians knew that a rebellion was brewing in the country, but certainly the press was not going to reveal it. There was no such thing as a free press, radio, or TV in Ethiopia. It did not take long for my wife and I to learn that Haile Selassie was Mr. Smith if the conversation about him was to be the least bit critical. As previously mentioned, the first week we were in our apartment we learned that our phone was tapped and a suspicious man in a car was parked on the street outside our apartment most of time. Our surveillance ended after my wife strongly protested to the telephone company, and of course it had satisfied itself that we were not spying.

A brief summary of progress made by Haile Selassie in modernizing Ethiopia: He made considerable progress in terms of increasing productivity, especially in agriculture. The best example was in cotton production where he used irrigation on a larger scale than had previously been the case. Of course he did this by allowing foreign firms in to produce the cotton and build up the manufacturing. It is difficult to tell what effect this had on production by Ethiopian farmers.

Selassie made some progress in manufacturing, particularly in cotton and sugar. Also a petroleum processing plant was set up but I am not sure where the oil processed in the plant came from. To the best of my knowledge, oil in sufficient quantity to justify a petroleum plant has not been found in Ethiopia. While I was there in 1972-74 the Tenneco Corporation had an exploratory group looking for oil and at the conclusion of their efforts the report was that sufficient oil was not found to drill wells. There was, however, considerable gas found. In fact there was enough gas to warrant a project to produce it on a commercial basis. I don't believe this has ever been carried out. Ethiopia does have considerable hydro electrical capabilities and some hydro electrical projects were put into operation during Haile Selassie's reign.

Haile Selassie was responsible for establishing an air line – national and international – in the country. Some improvements in the road situation were made due to the emperor's efforts, though most of this was done by the Italians during their five year attempt to occupy the country. By the turn of the century Ethiopia had almost eighteen hundred miles of road and only thirteen percent of that was paved. It must be admitted that much of Ethiopia is high country and road building is expensive and difficult. Haile Selassie is due some credit for road building but not much. The major piece of recent road building is the road that connects Addis Ababa with Nairobi Kenya, and it was completed after the emperor had been deposed in 1974. The rail line to Djibouti from Addis was arranged for and completed during the reign of Menelik II. Selassie is due credit for establishing the state run television in Ethiopia, and there were several newspapers in Addis but all were heavily censored by direction of the emperor.

As mentioned earlier, Haile Selassie was the first emperor to establish a constitution in 1931 and 1955. The 1955 constitution was an update of the 1931 constitution. As mentioned, both gave the emperor unlimited power and did nothing to create a more democratic government. In appearance the document resembled Western style constitutions, but the content was entirely different. Any actions or proposals by members of the bicameral parliament had to meet with the approval of Haile Selassie or he would veto them.

While I do not recall this complaint being mentioned relative to the attempted coup of 1960 it likely lurked in the background. Sufficient to say the coup took place when Haile Selassie was out of the country and it was spear headed by the Imperial Body Guard, a guard he had created. Selassie hurried back to Addis Ababa put down the coup with help from regular army. Supposedly his eldest son, Crown Prince Asfa Wossen, was implicated in the attempt but upon further investigation it was determined that he was not. It is still thought by many Ethiopians and others that he might have been involved. The process of change in Ethiopia stepped up after this attempted coup of 1960. The complaints and protest were about the need for land reform. The feudal system, with its many inequities, was being seriously questioned by the foreign trained students and other enlightened observers. Labor unions were becoming more aware of the inequities they experienced. Members of Parliament were complaining about their lack of influence or power to bring about needed changes. Like most everything in Ethiopia, change took place slowly and so it was with the situations mentioned above. But in 1974 the "pot boiled over" and the rule of an emperor dictatorship ended (more about this later).

More About Haile Selassie

Haile Selassie did bring about much central government control over the provinces. He caused all of the provinces to be ruled in his name by governor generals. Many of these governor generals resided in Addis Ababa while subordinates directed affairs in the provinces. One of the functions performed by the central controlled government was the collection of taxes. It was a function formerly performed by the lords and nobles in the provinces. Of course there was much objection to this on part of the ruling class in the provinces.

Haile Selassie did much to modernize the military forces of the country. With help from the British, Swedes, Israelis, and most importantly the United States, Haile Selassie was able to modernize the army. As early as 1960 the army included modern tanks, artillery batteries, antiaircraft batteries, and engineers. Most of this equipment came from the U.S. There was also a military mission from the U.S. as early as 1954. A military training college was established at Holetta near Addis Ababa to train officers and at the Haile Selassie Military Academy in Hararr.

The navy was not very strong. For one thing Ethiopia did not have a very long coast line to control, and after it lost Eritrea and its two major seaports at Masssawa and Assab, it was landlocked. Of course this did not happen while Haile Selassie was the emperor. When he was Emperor he managed to acquire, according to Hess, a United States seaplane tender, two torpedo boats of Yugoslav origin, five United States patrol boats, and two small landing craft, also from United States. There were a host of foreign countries that provided assistance in training the 210 officers and 1,000 seamen at the Naval School at Massawa. By contrast there was a force of 28,000 police equipped and trained by the Germans.

Travel was always a problem in Ethiopia due in part to the high plains and other rough terrain problems. Tewodros had early on recognized this and had attempted to work on the roads with some minor success, but it was more than he could accomplish in his shortened life. Haile Selassie recognized the problem. Before he could do much about the situation, as mentioned earlier, the Italians temporarily took over the country and forced Haile Selassie to take refuge in England for five years. During this time the Italians quickly realized the need to improve the road situation. In a short time roads were improved, bridges, tunnels, and overpasses were built. Had the Italians not been driven out it is likely they would have solved the road situation. Haile Selassie did continue to improve the roads but not as quickly nor as effectively as the Italians. He did however recognize that a modern Ethiopia needed to have its own airline, and especially so to supplement a road system such as existed in Ethiopia. He brought in instructors from the United States and established the Ethiopian Airline. It operated nationwide and internationally. It was a needed supplement to travel in Ethiopia, especially because of the long distances separating the major cities and towns from Addis Ababa, and the lack of good paved roads separating them.

How Does Haile Selassie Measure Up?

Haile Selassie moved the country ahead more than any other emperor. It is difficult to recall any sector of the economy in which improvements were not made – agriculture, manufacturing, imports, some exports, and electrical power. Social conditions were improved, especially in the establishment of schools and colleges. Training abroad was expanded. Relations with the national church were improved. Haile Selassie was able to break the hold of the Egyptian Coptic Church over the Ethiopian Church. It had been that way since the beginning of Christianity in Ethiopia, in the fourth century A.D. Ethiopia now had its own Buna (head of church). Haile Selassie had great success in securing funds and technical assistance from foreign countries. He made good start in modernizing his country, but in the end he failed. He failed because he persisted in maintaining a long outmoded feudal system. It is my personal opinion that Haile Selassie held on to power too long. He allowed a small group of selfish land owners, many from his own family, to influence him not to make the changes needed. On the removal of the feudal system I doubt he would have willingly ever agreed to that change. To do so would have relegated him a position of honorary emperor not a ruling emperor. And that would have been too much for his ego.

The feudal system that had lasted for over two thousand years was allowed to continue, but with some modifications imposed by the emperor to better control the larger land operators. A major modification was to pass an agricultural income tax law that stripped the legal right of land lords to tithe their tenants. This law was without teeth as the landlords refused to obey it throughout Ethiopia. Also petty landholders refused to allow their lands to be surveyed. The parliament did prevent the passage of major land reform bill, but in other matters before the Parliament, the emperor had his way. Haile Selassie created the Parliament and did so in a way that it served to merely ratify his programs. Quoting from Hess: *As one government official candidly admitted "We did not want a person who could work well in the Parliament and legislate proper laws. We wanted people to accept those laws which were to be legislated, and these laws could only get acceptance if they were discussed by the nobility and accepted by them first...We used them as instruments for the achievements of our plans and goals."* Of course Haile Selassie always assured the members that the laws proposed had been carefully vetted by experts and reviewed by responsible Ministers and the council of ministers before they were asked to approve them. This system applied to all forms of development, agriculture, manufacturing, road building, etc. Haile Selassie was an extremely clever ruler and did get many needed developments in operation, but in the end he also failed because he put loyalty ahead of all else. Ability was often viewed as a handicap. It was better to have a loyal member than a wise one who would question the emperor's decisions and refuse to go along. In time, autocratic rule helped to bring him down.

Thus far I have relied upon Robert L. Hess, a very reliable historian and author of *"Ethiopia The Modernization of Autocracy"* for much of the factual information on Haile Selassie, but now I will switch to a book titled *"The Emperor"*. This book is by a Polish writer Ryszard Kapuscinski, originally published in 1978 and translated from Polish by William Brand in 1983. It was published in the United States by Vintage International. Note especially the date this book was originally published, 1978. The significance of this date is that it was published while Ethiopia was being ruled by a communistic government headed by Mengistu Haile-Mariam. The data in the book had been obtained by the author shortly after the coup that brought down the emperor. It was an act of courage on the part of the author and those who collaborated with him. Had they been caught, the consequences would have been serious. It could have meant death for all, or certainly death for the Ethiopians and expulsion for the author. After reading the book I have concluded the author wanted to present a story of how Haile Selassie ruled Ethiopia, especially in the last few years, and why he was removed as dictator.

Hear the story: The story really begins back in 1963 when a meeting of the presidents of independent African nations was taking place. Haile Selassie had furbished up Addis Ababa. The beggars had been rounded up and hauled out of the city. Dead bodies had been removed from the streets. Addis was still a relatively small city with many buildings unfinished and muddy side streets. Work was still going on with gangs of laborers supervised by Armenians. A foreman carrying a long cane circulated among them and prodded them on.

Meanwhile, back at the emperor's palace a huge reception was taking place. Over three thousand people with different colored invitations were invited and fed from a variety of menus. Wine and caviar shipped in from Europe was served. Entertainment from Hollywood was brought in. It was indeed a lavish party. Nasser from Egypt was there as well as many other distinguished guests. There was one dark skinned waiter for every four guests and there were tons of priceless silver. It was reported that some of this silver disappeared as mementos carried away in pockets and pocket books.

By way of contrast the author, one of the invitees, slipped outside to get a bit of fresh air. He noted that the beggars just outside the huge kitchen were devouring the scraps as they were being brought back to the kitchen and thrown out by the dish washers.

The party was a great success and the presidents began leaving next day. Conditions in these relatively new countries had not settled enough to allow the presidents to leave their capitols without fear of being displaced in their absence. Now it was time for the foreign correspondents to file their stories, and they were having trouble doing so. Their Ethiopian contact was Teferra Gebrewold head of the Ministry of Information and he was doing what he could. Volumes of communiqués so overloaded the lines that it was not possible to get them out in a timely manner, and this did not make a group of tired reporters happy. They threatened to go to the emperor. To do so would surely jeopardize the Minister of Information, likely to the extent of actually causing him to lose his job. Some of the cooler heads among the reporters, especially the author of *"The Emperor"* prevailed and decided against going to Haile Selassie.

Setting

Had this not happened the book, *The Emperor,* might not have been written because it was this minister of information who later was able to round up those who were to provide eye witness information contained in the book. These informants ranged from ministers to lowly servants who were in position to observe what actually went on daily in Haile Selassie's palace. Over the years since the 1963 meeting, the author had revisited Addis Ababa a number of times. He always maintained a good relationship with his friend Teferra Gebrewold, the Minister of Information. When Kapuscinski needed a friend who knew the reliable informants and could get them to meet with him, Teferra was there. The gathering of information must have begun around1976 or 1977 based on the book being published in 1978. My wife and I left Ethiopia in early March of 1974 and there were group gatherings, marches, rocks being thrown at cars, and other such activities, but no armed jeeps running around shooting and killing people. Let us now hear the story of the fall of Haile Selassie from Kapuscinski book.

The author states that his purpose is to *"recapture the world that had been wiped away by the machine guns of the Fourth Division."* By world he means the operations that took place in the palace before leaders of the coup (a group of military men who were from that division and had its support) had overthrown the emperor. This would enable the author to determine why he was overthrown. It also serves as a check on what the historians have said about Haile Selassie and why he was ousted.

More About Haile Selassie

The author avoided detection and capture by soldiers of the Fourth Division. They were constantly patrolling the streets of Addis Ababa in American-made jeeps. Their machine guns were fired at frequent intervals – sometimes at people, buildings or just up in the air. The drivers paid no attention to traffic rules, driving recklessly. People walking the streets were doing what they could to stay away from these rebels. I fail to see the reason for this display except to show they were in control and to impress the crowds with their bravado.

As one can see it was dangerous to walk or ride the streets, but there was another threat – the fetasha in Amharic meaning to search. The authorities ordered a complete fetasha to get things under control. There were at least two sides to the revolution and people did not know what side the other person was on, thus the excuse for the fetashas. And complete it was. People were being searched night and day on the street in buildings, in offices, on the highways at the checkpoints, anywhere and by anybody. The searches were especially directed at foreigners. Anyone could search them because they did not know who had the right to search and who did not, and to ask only made things worse. As the author put it, *"Guys in rags with sticks, who don't say anything, but only stop us and hold out their arms, which is the signal for us to do the same: get ready to be searched. They take everything out of our briefcases and pockets, look at it, act surprised, screw up their faces, nod their head, whisper advice to each other. They frisk us: back, stomach, legs, and shoes. And then what? Nothing, we can go on until the next spreading of the arms, until the next fetasha. The next one may be only a few steps on, and the whole thing starts all over again. The searchers never give you an acquittal, a general clearance, absolution."* These street searches are bad, but the road searches are worse, and on a trip, even a short one they are numerous. You have to get out, the luggage is torn open, strewn about until it is in pieces spread out on the ground, and thoroughly inspected. Then the passengers are thoroughly searched, and the items on the ground are tossed back in the luggage all rumpled. This same procedure will happen at the next checkpoint, likely only a short distance down the road. The army will sometimes conduct fetashas by blocking off a quarter of a city looking for ammunition dumps, underground printing presses, and anarchists.

Palace Activities

Kapuscinski (the author) developed a simple plan to obtain the information he wanted to convey, the story of how Haile Selassie ruled Ethiopia just prior to his removal as dictator. To repeat, it is amazing that the author was able to locate, with the help of a top Ethiopian palace official, these key people who were so conversant with Haile Selassie's activities. And more amazing they were able to provide the information while the Dergue headed by Mengistu Haile-Mariam controlled Ethiopia.

The plan begins with the servant (identified only by initials L.C.) who responds to the emperor's buzzer. The palace day begins. The emperor seemed mad that he had to waste time on sleep. He was an early riser. The servant, a keen observer, noted that the emperor "never showed the slightest sign of irritation, nervousness, anger, rage, or frustration. It seemed he never knew such states." Good politicians always try to control these emotions. It seemed that as conditions grew worse, the emperor traveled more. This likely provided him an escape from the unpleasant situations now taking place in the palace.

Next, Haile Selassie listens to informer reports. It is observed that the night breeds dangerous conspiracies. Haile Selassie knows that what happens during the night is more important than what happens during the day. He can see what goes on during the day but it is not possible to see what happens during the dark of night. All reports are made verbally and it is noted that this is because the emperor's reading ability is said to be limited due to his lack of formal education (mentioned elsewhere in this book). Also this permits the emperor to shape the report as he sees fit. This same philosophy was applied to written decisions. The minister of the pen, who was the closest confidant of the emperor and enjoyed enormous power, was always at the emperor's side during all official functions. He took down all the emperor's orders and instructions. It was noted that the emperor's voice was very low and was only audible to the minister of the pen. This permitted the minister to shape the orders and reports as he saw fit. For those decisions that appeared wise the emperor looked great. For those not so great the minister could be blamed. Incidentally the emperor never signed any documents.

Following the reports of the informers, the emperor would take his morning walk beginning in the park. As he entered the park the head of the palace spies, Kedir, joins him to give his report. He trails a step behind the emperor talking all the while. Quoting who met whom, where and what they talked about, against whom they are forming alliances, and whether or not one could call it a conspiracy. Kedir also reports on the military cryptography department. This department is a part of Kedir's office, which decodes the communications that pass among the divisions...it's good to be sure that no subversive thoughts are hatching there. His distinguished highness asks no questions, makes no comments. He walks and listens. At times he feeds the lions or watches the lions and leopards. Then he continues on listening to Kedir's report. At some point he bows his head, a signal to Kedir that the session has ended and Kedir bows and disappears, never turning his back on the emperor.

His next meeting is with the Minister of Industry and Commerce, Makonen Habte-Wald who emerges from behind a tree. He falls in, a step behind the emperor. Makonen reports on the basis of his own network of informers. He does so to partially satisfy his own passion for intrigue and partially to ingratiate himself with his majesty. He briefs the emperor on what happened last night and the emperor nods his head, a sign for Makonen to terminate his report. Makonen bows and retreats backward.

Next, as though rising up from nowhere, springs Asha Walde-Mikael, a devoted confidant, who supervises the government political police. He competes with Solomon's Palace intelligence and battles hard against private intelligence networks such as Makonen Habte-Wald. It was noted that these intelligence people lived a hard and dangerous life. They looked tired and worked under feverish stress. There were times when they had nothing of consequence to report but felt they must give some type of report. This could get them in trouble. The emperor had the upper hand. He was getting information on the same subject from more than one source and could make up his mind as to who was correct and could undo those whom he thought were deceiving him with a wave of his hand. But to the emperor it was imperative that he have the correct information. Also he never questioned the reports or asked question. He did not want to cause the reporter to change his report because he thought the emperor wanted to hear it different from what it actually was. The author states it this way: *"His highness wanted to receive the reports in a pure state, because if he asked questions or expressed opinions the informant would obligingly adjust his report to meet the emperor's expectations".*

After the emperor has heard from all his informants he then begins to mentally sort out what he has heard. Usually much of what he has heard is of little importance. The author reflects on the emperor's mental abilities and how he uses them to rule. Quoting: *"The emperor ponders. Now is the time to lay out strategies and tactics to solve the puzzles of personality, to plan his next move on chessboard of power. He thinks deeply about what was contained in the informant's reports. Little of importance; they usually report on each other... his mind is a computer that retains every detail; even the smallest datum will be remembered. There was no personnel office in the Palace, no dossiers full of personal information. All this the emperor carried in his mind, all the most important files about the elite. I see him now as he walks, stops, walks again, and lifts his head upward as though absorbed in prayer. Some speculation by the author or perhaps from the minister of the pen follows: O God, save me from those who crawling on their knees, hide a knife that they would like to sink in my back. But how can God help? All the people surrounding the emperor are just like that–on their knees, and with knives. It's is never comfortable on the summits. An icy wind always blows, and everyone crouches, watchful lest his neighbor hurl him from the precipice." – Excerpts from book "The Emperor," Pgs.6-12.*

The minister of the pen, Teferra Gebrewold previously mentioned as the person who provided the names of the Ethiopian informers also provided some insights on the emperor's ability and method of ruling Ethiopia. Quoting Teferra: *"The factions in the palace were the aristocrats, the bureaucrats, and the so called 'personal people.' The aristocrats, made up of the great landowners and conservative in the extreme, grouped themselves mostly in the Crown Council, and leader was Prince Kassa, who has since been executed. The bureaucrats most enlightened and most progressive since some had a higher education filled the ministries and imperial offices. The faction of the 'personal people' was a peculiarity of our regime, created by the emperor himself."* The personal people were selected by the emperor from the common people in the various provinces. How they came to his attention is not clear. The Emperor from time to time did visit the provinces and there were always mobs of people around him. It is likely that some of the emperor's trusted advisors brought potential prospects to his attention. Others, by whatever means, caught the emperors attention and were personally selected. The important aspect is that once selected they were brought in to the palace and mixed with the aristocrats and bureaucrats. They served the emperor *"with an indescribable eagerness and were, of course despised and hated by the aristocrats and bureaucrats. These were the people he trusted."* For example, his minister of pen was one of the 'personal people', as was the political police and the superintendence of the palace.* *Excerpt from "The Emperor", Pg.30.*

The following excerpt will give one a good idea as to how detailed the emperor was in running the country. *"Not only did the emperor decide on all promotions, but he also communicated with each one personally. He alone. He filled the post at the summit of the hierarchy, and also its lower and middle levels. He appointed the postmasters, headmasters of the schools, police constables, all the most ordinary office employees, estate managers, brewery directors, managers of hospitals and hotels. And let me say it again, he chose them personally...The emperor supervised even the most lowly assignment, because the source of power was not the state or any institution, but most personally his benevolent highness."* How important a rule that was? What amazes me is the amount of detail the emperor handles, and seems to handle well.* *"The Emperor," Pg. 31.*

During this period his minister of pen was Walde Giyorgis and the informants were trying to tell the emperor he was the most perverse, corrupt, repulsive personality ever to have been supported by the floors of our palace, but his highness would not listen. Finally, the arrogance of the Minister led him to participate in a meeting with a conspiratorial group and the palace security service reported it to the emperor. The emperor waited for Walde to report this to him but he did not. At the hour of assignments, the emperor demoted the second highest ranking official in the empire to the post of a minor functionary in a backward province. He had violated the principal of loyalty, and there were others who ranked high such as Prince Imru. Imru violated the loyalty principle by announcing some land reform measures without consulting the emperor. The emperor actually favored land reform but the Prince was not giving the emperor the credit, a serious mistake. The Prince was exiled from the country for twenty years.

Fall of the Dynasty

According to the book *"The Emperor"* the fall began in 1973 when a British journalist, Jonathan Dimbleby visited Ethiopia, specifically the northern part. There were no objections as he had visited Ethiopia before and had only good things to say. This time was different. A short time after he returned to England the Ethiopian Ambassador reported that Mr. Dimbleby had produced and shown a film titled *Ethiopia: The Unknown Famine on London TV*. The film showed thousands of people dying of starvation with skeletons lying all around. This was contrasted with pictures of wines and caviar arriving at the palace from Europe and the emperor serving meat to his dogs from a silver platter. Dimbleby put deaths at a hundred thousand with more to come. A great scandal broke out in London. His royal highness, Haile Selassie, was condemned.

What To Do?

Many of those around the emperor could not understand what the fuss was all about. There had been famines before and there had been no particular disturbance raised. A plane load of European journalists took off from London to see what was happening in Ethiopia. When they arrived, questions immediately arose as to what to do with them. Some Ethiopian officials wanted to forbid them to go to northern areas where the famine was taking place. Others decided that to do so would make the emperor look bad since he had agreed that food and medicines were needed. Some tried to dissuade them from going due to almost impassable roads and bandits along the way. Meanwhile the missionaries, nurses, and students were most upset that those in need were not being helped. It was noted by those in the affected areas that there were thousands dying right next door to markets and stores full of food. True, the area had a short crop and the peasants had to give their entire crops to landowners. Then the speculators stepped in and raised the prices.

The Unexpected Happens

Some of the students travelled to affected areas and took pictures of the people starving next to markets full of food and made them available to the foreign journalists. Other students in Addis marched the streets shouting obscenities, denouncing the corruption, and mounting cries for indictments. The police clubbed and arrested them. What was happening in Addis would have passed in a short time had it not been for an unrelated and unplanned event – a fashion show organized by the American Peace Corps. The emperor recognized the rebellious students had a proper venue for their protest and they took full advantage of it. They gathered a huge crowd and headed for the palace.

The following quotation from the book titled *"The Emperor"* seems to sum up the results so well: *"And from that moment on they never let themselves be driven back to their homes. They held meetings, they stormed implacably and vehemently, they did not yield again. And General Shibeshi was tearing his hair out because not even to him had it occurred that a revolution could start at a fashion show." *Pg.116, "The Emperor".*

Hailu, the son of one of the notables and a malcontent student is explaining to his father: *"But that is exactly how it looked to us. This is the beginning of the end for all of you. We cannot live like this any longer. This death up north and the lies of the court have covered us with shame. The country is drowning in corruption. People are dying of hunger, ignorance, and barbarity everywhere. We feel ashamed of this country. And yet we have no other country, we have to dig it out ourselves. Your palace has compromised us before the world, and such a palace can no longer exist. We know there is unrest in the army and unrest in the city, and now we cannot back down." *Pg. 117,"The Emperor".*

*"Yes...among those noble, very irresponsible people, one was struck by the deep feelings of shame about the state of the fatherland. For them there extended only the twentieth century, or perhaps even this twenty-first century is waiting for, in which blessed justice will reign. Nothing else suited them anymore, everything else irritated them. They decided to arrange the world so they would be able to look back at it with contentment. Oh well...young people, very young people!" * Pg.117, ""The Emperor"–This appears to be a comment by Hailu's father.*

The emperor seemed to be unaware of the unusual situation in the country. He decided to take a trip to Eritrea to see his grandson who was the fleet commander and have him take him on a short cruise on the flagship. However, one of the engines would not start and the cruise was called off. A French ship was in the port of Massawa and the French admiral invited him on board for dinner, never mind the uproar over the starving people. The next day he summoned the notables from the north. They had been accused by the missionaries and nurses of speculating and stealing from the starving, and conferred high distinction on them to prove their innocence. Back in Addis the finance minister, desiring to enrich the imperial treasury, ordered that high custom fees be paid on the food and medicines being shipped in by foreign countries donating these items.

On a personal note, my wife and I had this happen to us when we had some items shipped in by our church while we were in Addis about this same time). The minister of commerce objected to the minister of finance ordering hungry people. To pay high custom fees Haile Selassie accepted the denunciation from the minister of commerce but did not reprimand the minister of finance with a single harsh word. The countenance of the emperor showed satisfaction. This aid offered by the foreign countries appeared to the emperor to be critical of his development program and he showed his resentment, never mind the thousands of starving people.

The next sign of trouble was in January of 1974 when a report reached the emperor that General Beleta Abebe had been arrested by soldiers at Gode barracks and he was being forced to eat the same food they were. Further, the food was so obviously rotten that he was getting sick. The emperor sent in an airborne unit to get the general and take him to the hospital. It seems that in spite of the all the emperor had done to improve the food situation, the generals had been putting the money in their pockets and making sizeable fortunes. The emperor however did not reprimand any of the generals, but ordered the soldiers at Gode be dispersed. The situation quieted down for a short time only to come up again in the Negele garrison in Sidamo province when the soldiers started a rebellion an arrested their officers. This time the problem was unsanitary water in the enlisted men's well and they decided to drink from the officers well.

No action was taken in Negele due to the unrest taking place in the capitol – a mutiny in the vicinity of the palace – and a number of other disturbing events. The minister of commerce raised the price of gas, taxi drivers went on strike, teachers go on strike, five high school students caused a disturbance and were caught by police. They were sent tumbling down a hill with police shooting at them. Three were killed and two wounded - there is no time to take any action on affair at garrison in Sidamo. The enlisted men are drinking from the officer's well to their hearts content. The university students get back in the fray and head back to the palace. The police set the dogs on them, shoot, and arrest them. Nothing stops them until the emperor calls off the increase in gas. Even this does not quiet the situation.

While all this is going on, news comes in that the Second Division in Eritrea has rebelled and occupied Asmara, arrested their general, locked up the provincial governor, and made a godless proclamation over the radio. They demand justice, pay raises, and human funerals. It seems that officers were given funerals but enlisted men were left to the vultures and hyenas. The following day the navy rebels and the emperor's grandson has to flee. The air force mutinies followed by biggest and most important of the army divisions, the Fourth located in Addis Ababa. Conditions are about as bad as they can get.

The Emperor Acts

Recognizing that strong action was needed to quiet the rebellion taking place in the country, the emperor announced a pay raise for the soldiers, and ordered Premier Aklilu and his government to resign. The dignitary Endelkachew, a liberal blessed with an ability to speak well, was appointed to head the government. This action by the emperor did nothing to quiet the street noise. Demonstrations, students, and worker complaints all continued to sound off. Another army mutiny takes place. This time it is the Third Division stationed in Ogaden. Only the Imperial Guard showed any loyalty.

Residents of the palace were divided as to what should be done. Zera Yakob was a possible successor to his throne. Yakob was the son of Prince Asfa Wossen whose father was Haile Selassie. The prince was said to be permanently paralyzed and living in a Geneva hospital. The truth of this is questionable. There are Ethiopians living in USA who think the prince was well and living in U.S. at the time). In any event, the emperor's choice was not very popular with those residing at the palace. Members of the Crown Council started to complain and protest. They did not want to serve under one so young. It was a humiliation to their advanced age and many achievements. Other suggestions to head the country included Tenene Work, daughter of the emperor, and Prince Makonen, another grandson of the emperor who was being educated in an officer's school in the U.S.

While all the intrigue over the succession was taking place the army entered the town during the night and arrested all the ministers of the old Aklilu government. The group included Aklilu and two hundred generals and high ranking officers known to be loyal to the ruler. Even the chief of the general staff, Assefa Ayena, was arrested. Ayena was the officer who had saved the throne during the December events by destroying the Neway brothers and defeating the imperial guard. *Pg.127-128, "The Emperor".*

There was utter confusion in the palace. The emperor listened to all sides and all were given comfort and praise no matter what they were suggesting. The residents of the palace were a bit amazed to see the emperor act in this manner and some expressed what most were thinking, that the emperor must have lost his mind. At one point during this time, the emperor decided to announce his successor. Dignitaries were gathered in the great throne chamber And the Emperor in a very quiet voice announced: that bearing in mind his advanced age and the evermore-often heard call of the Lord of Host, he was nominating his ...grandson Zera Yakob...This was the twenty-year old son of Prince Asfa Wossen, the only remaining son of the emperor.

During most of the days now the emperor wore his army uniform with ribbons. This was because officers of the army, especially from Fourth Division were paying him visits almost daily. Also a group of palace residents were being taken away to prison by the army almost daily. The emperor never complained about the actions of the military and was always sure to praise the military. Conversely, the military always gave the impression that their actions were being taken at the direction of the emperor. At this point the new government was not sure that it had reached a point where it's acceptance by the people was superior to that of the emperor. Until it was, it preferred to continue looking as though it was carrying out the will of the people at direction of the emperor. The masters of the new government were playing a waiting game. It was easy to understand their actions, but those of the emperor were more difficult to understand. Either he was not playing with a full deck or he deliberately chose to go along with the military in order to satisfy his ego or lust for power. One event that took place in May of 1974 seems to justify the idea that ego was upper most important to him. The war veterans organized a demonstration of loyalty for the emperor in front of the palace. He came out on the balcony and thanked the army for its unshakable loyalty, and wished it further prosperity and success. Contrast this to his negative reactions to his daughters request to punish the army.

Not long after this event some of the palace group came up with the idea of a birthday celebration for the emperor on his 82nd birthday. Some said it should have been his 92nd because at one time his majesty had subtracted some years from his record. The important thing was to have a party stir up some life and they tried. Unfortunately, his birthday came on a chilly rainy day and when his majesty came out on the balcony to speak there was no crowd, only a handful of soaked depressed dignitaries, some palace servants, and a few soldiers from the Imperial Guard were present. His speech was short. He expressed compassion for the starving provinces, and that he would continue his program of development of the country. As always, he thanked the army for its loyalty. His voice was barely above a whisper, and some tears were observed. It seemed to some that the end was approaching.

At this point in *"The Emperor"*, the situation between Haile Selassie and his opponents (the Derge) is summarized as it appears in the summer of 1974. In my estimation the summary is accurate and eloquent. I shall use major parts of the material on pages 139-143 (shown in italics): *"It is the summer of 1974 - a contest great is going on between two shrewd antagonists: the venerable Emperor and the officers from the Derge. For the officers it is a game of hide-and-seek: they are trying to encircle the ancient monarch in his own palace, in his lair. And the Emperor? His plan is subtle, but let's wait, because in a moment we will come to know his thoughts. The other players in this struggle between the rebels (Dergue) are the Jailers, Talkers, and Floaters. In the book "The Emperor they are described as follows:*

> *"Helpless and frightened, dignitaries and favorites rampage through the corridors of the Palace. We must remember that the Palace was a nest of mediocrity, a collection of second rate people, and in time of crisis such people lose their heads and think of nothing but saving their own skins. Mediocrity is dangerous: when it feels itself threatened it becomes ruthless. Such precisely are the Jailers, who are not up to much beyond cracking the whip and spilling blood. Fear and hatred blind them, and the basest forces prod them to action: meanness, fierce egotism, fear of losing their privileges and being condemned. Dialogue with such people is impossible, senseless. The Talkers are the second group- people of good will but defensive by nature, wavering, compliant, an incapable of transcending the patterns of Palace thinking. They get beaten worse of all from every side, shoved out of the way and destroyed. They try to move about in a context that has been torn in half, in which the two and passed them by. About the Floaters nothing can be said. They drift along wherever the current drags them, a school of small-fry carried away, pulled in all directions, fighting, striving for even the meanest kind of survival."*

The paragraph that follows analyses the group of young officers that oppose Haile Selassie and the palace groups. It appears that Haile Selassie constitutes most of the opposition feared by the officers.

Quoting from The Emperor, Pg.140

"That's the fauna of the palace, against which the group of young officers is acting-bright, intelligent men, ambitious and embittered patriots conscious of the terrible state of affairs in their fatherland, of the stupidity and helplessness of the elite, of corruption and depravity, the misery and humiliating dependence of the country on stronger states. They themselves, as part of the Imperial army, belong to the lower ranks of the elite; they, too have taken advantage of privileges, so it is not poverty - which they have never experienced directly - that goads them to action, but rather the feeling of moral shame and responsibility. They have weapons, and they decide to make the best use of them." The conspiracy begins in the headquarters of the Fourth Division in the strict secrecy as they fear any slight leak might bring repressions and executions. In time the conspiracy finds its way into other garrisons, and after that the ranks of the police.

The drought was the major event that brought on the confrontation between the army and the palace. The seriousness of the drought was overplayed. The real cause was the fact that the peasants were virtually robbed of the grain they produced by means of an unjust contract between the land lords and the peasants. Once the grain was on the market, the price was doubled. This price was beyond the means of the peasants. In areas outside the drought areas abundant grain crops were produced. Some of this grain was moved into markets in the drought areas, but at prices based on grain produced in the short crop areas. Hundreds of thousands of peasants starved next to abundantly stocked granaries. Grain was also exported to markets outside Ethiopia while peasants in Ethiopia were starving. To add insult to injury "On the orders of local Dignitaries, the police finished off whole clans of still living human skeletons." It is little wonder that the military stepped in to oppose Haile Selassie and the upper class dignitaries, especially when the army surely contained many men not long removed from the peasant population. After a short period of bewilderment, shock, and hesitation, Haile Selassie began to realize he was losing his most important instrument, the army.* *Covered in "The Emperor", Pgs 140-141.*

Moments of Doubt

At the beginning the Dergue acted in darkness, hidden in conspiracy; they didn't know how much the army would back them. They had workers and students behind them-that was important, but a majority of generals and higher ranking officers were against the conspirators, and it was the generals who still commanded, still gave the orders. Step by step – that was the tactic of this revolution. If they had come out openly and at once, the disoriented part of the army might have refused to support them or might have even destroyed them. There would have been a repeat performance of the drama of 1960, when the army fired on the army and the palace was thus preserved for another thirteen years. In any case, the Dergue itself lacked unity; sure everyone wanted to liquidate the palace, they wanted to change the anachronistic, worn out, helplessly vegetating system, but quarrels went on about what to do about the person of the monarch. The emperor had created around himself a myth, the force and vitality of which it was impossible to ascertain. He was well-liked in the world, full of personal charm, universally respected. What's more he was the head of the church, the chosen one of God, the ruler of men's souls. Raise one's hand against him? It always ended in the anathema and the gallows.

*The members of the Dergue were people of great courage, and also to some extent desperadoes, since they recalled afterwards that even when they had decided to stand up against the emperor, they still didn't believe in their own chances of success. Perhaps Haile Selassie knew something about the doubts and divisions that consumed the Dergue; after all, he possessed an extraordinary well developed intelligence service." In summary Haile Selassie seemed to understand that he could no longer withstand the struggle with the army. He began to yield and finally gave up his task of ruling. "He feigned his existence, but the ones closest to him knew he really was not doing anything; he wasn't in action." * The Emperor, Pgs. 141-142.*

Military Moves In

His associates were confused by the passive action of Haile Selassie. They offered him their suggestions and he listened. He nodded his approval and praised them; offered comfort an encouragement, but no action took place. He just remained aloof and above the conflict. He seemed mainly interested in what would happen to him.

Maybe, since he was old and feeble, he would be spared. The military cautiously decided to move up their actions. First they dismantled the elite, they gradually emptied the palace and moved the dignitaries to the jail of the Fourth Division. Here there were long lines of limousines with the wives and relatives of prisoners bringing food and clothing to them. Cautiously looking on were groups of spectators who were excited and curious about what they were seeing. The street is not yet aware of events taking place at the palace. There the emperor is still in his Palace and the military is planning its next move.

At this stage a rather amusing incident takes place in the palace. The emperor had summoned his Swedish physicians to the palace but for some reason they had delayed their appearance. The order went out from the emperor for the inhabitants to show up for calisthenics. The order extolled the value of taking exercises and staying fit. With the palace in a turmoil, it did seem a bit strange for the residents be taking exercises. Of course this just suited the military who was there to take all the residents in to custody. To make it a little more difficult for the military an order went out to break the residents down into several groups. The military had little trouble overcoming this problem and continued take away residents. Strangely dignitaries from over the empire continued to come to the palace seeking refuge from military officials in the provinces. They refused to believe the emperor had lost his power to help them. As they came in the military from the Fourth Division had a daily patrol come to the palace and take away residents. By early August nearly all the residents had been taken and the palace was nearly in shambles. The residents were wrapping themselves in palace curtains at night to keep warm, and as the curtains became scarce, disputes were breaking out. The residents argued over who was entitled to have a curtain, or more important *should* the curtains and draperies be taken down. It should be noted that Haile Selassie was always in uniform with medals. He would converse with the dignitaries and offer them hope and symphony. At same time he would compliment the military on how well they were doing their job. The daily military patrols had the palace ceremony officials call for a meeting of all dignitaries and then a list of those it wanted was read off and those people were taken off to jail. In last days before all the residents – save the emperor and his personal servant – were taken to jail. It was impossible to tell how many residents there were in the palace and this made it impossible for the cook to know how many to prepare food for. Some day residents were happy, and some days they weren't. It was strange how people would get upset over the quantity and quality of food when their very lives were at stake.

Haile Selassie – Good and Bad

I mentioned earlier that I would discuss some of the negative aspects of Haile Selassie's character in the latter part of the book. At that point I had not come across an excellent summary of his character as presented by the author of *"The Emperor"*. This summary is presented on pages 101 and 102 of *"The Emperor"*. The attempt to assassinate the emperor in 1960 has been discussed earlier on, but the author's summary grows out of it and begins when imperial guard commander Mengistu Neway comes to the university to address the students as to why the attempt was made on Haile Selassies life. You will recall the imperial guard opposed the emperor and that he was saved when the regular army took sides with the emperor. *"One of Haile Selassie's most trusted officers represented the emperor – a divine being, with supernatural attributes – as a man who tolerated corruption in the palace, defended a backward system, and accepted the misery of millions of his subjects. That day the fight began, and the university never again knew peace...lasting almost fourteen years, engulfed scores of victims and – ended only with the overthrow of the emperor."*

Haile Selassie – Last Days of a Dynasty

"In those years there existed two images of Haile Selassie. One known to international opinion presented the emperor as a rather exotic, gallant monarch, distinguished by indefatigable energy, a sharp mind, and profound sensitivity. A man who made a stand against Mussolini, recovered his empire and his throne, and had ambitions of developing his country and playing an important role in the world. The other image, formed gradually by a critical and initially small segment of Ethiopian opinion, showed the monarch as a ruler committed to defending his power at any cost. A man who was above all a great demagogue and theatrical paternalist who used words and gestures to mask the corruption and servility of a ruling elite that he had created and coddled. And, as often happens, both these images were correct...to some he was full of charm, while among others he provoked hatred. He ruled a country that knew only the cruelest methods of fighting for power (or of keeping it), in which free elections were replaced by poison and the dagger, discussions by shooting and the gallows. He was a product of this tradition, and he himself fell back upon it. Yet at same time he understood that there was an impossibility to it...but he could not change the system that kept him in power, and for him power came first. Hence the flights into demagoguery, into ceremony, into speeches about development - all so very empty in this country of oppressive misery and ignorance. He was a most amiable personage, a shrewd politician, a tragic father, a pathological miser. He condemned innocence to death and pardoned guilt..."

It should be remembered when trying to sum up the good and the evil in Haile Selassie, that he is the product of over two thousand years of dynastic rule. This type of rule was typical in European countries, but was abandoned much earlier than in Ethiopia. The reasons for its termination in Europe were much the same as those mentioned in Ethiopia, unfairness to multitudes of people who were at the bottom of the economic ladder. My opinion of Haile Selassie, before I examined his life in some detail, was very similar to the one described as International opinion. Now that I have delved deeper, I have to agree with the author of *"The Emperor"*. But having done so, I am still impressed with Haile Selassie and what he was able to accomplish – particularly in his last 15 years when he became obsessed in the modernization of Ethiopia. He was able to persuade so many European countries and the United States to provide technical and financial help for that purpose. The last two years of this 15 year period, I was in Ethiopia and saw first-hand what was taking place. What I did not know was how fierce the struggle was to oust Haile Selassie, nor did I understand how deep rooted the class system was. This was exemplified by the dynasty that had lasted for over two thousand years in that country.

Haile Selassie – Last Days of a Dynasty

Returning to the palace situation, the military was still making daily visits to the palace and taking away dignitaries, but one last attempt was made to save the day. The lawyers showed up with a revised constitution to present to his majesty. It had been changed to take away all the real power of the emperor. It would convert the autocratic Empire into a constitutional monarchy. This would strip away any real power from his majesty as was the case in Great Britain. The Jailers opposed this idea, and the Talkers favored it as a last chance to save any remaining power for the emperor. While they were arguing over the matter the military heard about it. They came in and took the document away from the lawyers and the squabbling Jailers and Talkers, and that was the end of the matter.

In August of 1974 the removal of dignitaries had about come to an end. For the first time the name of the officer who apparently headed the group making the decisions (a committee of one hundred and twenty delegates and known as the Dergue) was Mengistu Haile Mariam. At this time of final clearance of top officials, Haile Selassie's inner circle of officials consisted of a commander of the imperial guard, his aide-de-camp, the Premier, the Minister of Highest Privileges, and perhaps twenty others. Also the Crown Council was dissolved. It seems that when the palace troubles began, the situation became so time consuming that Haile Selassie had to turn over some of his duties of dispensing privileges to the Minister of Highest Privileges. This was a mistake that Haile Selassie seldom made, to misjudge the loyalty of an appointee. He would see the consequences later.

Meanwhile, the people on the street demanded that those responsible be brought to justice, even to point of hanging them. When the Dergue realized its propaganda program was working well, it decided the time was right to remove the emperor from the palace. Before this was actually done however, the matter of money in the palace and elsewhere came up. Some military officers visited the palace and demanded the emperor give them all the money. When the emperor demurred they ripped up a large rug displaying a floor covered with dollar bills. The officers tallied up the amount and had Haile Selassie sign for it. They left the palace and his majesty had his servant take all the money out one the drawers and conceal it in the pages of numerous religious books. The next day the officers returned and demanded more money and the emperor opened the drawer and showed it was empty. Almost immediately the officers picked up the bible and other religious books and shook them while the money rolled out. I expect those officers had somehow observed the money being concealed in the books the previous day. Of course a servant may have been guilty of betraying the emperor. The officers then had the emperor draw up a check on a Swiss bank for sizeable sum and sign it, but this check was never cashed. It is doubtful if the money stashed away by Haile Selassie has ever been located and returned to the Ethiopian treasury. I say this in spite of the many attempts made by the government that came in after Haile Selassie's ouster.

Around the end of August 1974, the Dergue decided the time had come to nationalize the emperor's palaces (all fifteen of them), and his private enterprises, such as his brewery, bus company, mineral water factory, and rug factory. On a personal note my wife and I purchased several nice rugs that were woven in the rug factory.

After the nationalization procedure, the next act by the Dergue was to dethrone the emperor. Just prior to this several officers had come to the palace and informed the emperor's servant that a film would be shown that evening. They said the emperor might like to see it and he was to tell the emperor about it. The film was Jonathan Dimbleby's on the famine in the northern part of Ethiopia. Strangely, the emperor sat quietly through the entire film. It was the Ethiopian New Year's Eve and the servant lit the candles all through the palace and Haile Selassie and the servant remained up all night. At day break they heard a great commotion outside the palace. It was caused by the throbbing of motors and the clanking of tank treads on the asphalt. Three officers entered the palace and made their way to the emperor's chamber. After bowing to the emperor they proceeded to read the act of dethronement as follows. I must mention that the act was also published later in the press and on the radio. The act was as follows: *"Even though the people treated the throne in good faith as a symbol of unity, Haile Selassie took advantage of its authority, dignity, and honor for his own personal ends. As a result, the country found itself in a state of poverty and disintegration. Moreover, an eighty-two year old monarch, because of his age, is incapable of meeting his responsibilities. Therefore His Imperial Majesty, Haile Selassie, is being deposed September 12, 1974, and power assumed by the Provisional Military Committee. Ethiopia above all." "The Emperor", Pg.161.*

After the act was read to him the emperor expressed his thanks to everyone and stated *"The army had never disappointed him, and added if the revolution is good for the people then he, too, supports the revolution and would not oppose the dethronement."* At that point the officer, a major, asks the former emperor to follow us to a Volkswagen. At this point Haile Selassie expresses his first sign of anger. *"You can't be serious"* he bridled. *"I'm supposed to go like this"?* He then fell silent and sat down in the back seat of the Volkswagen. He was taken to Menlik's Palace and placed under guard around the clock. The soldiers who guarded him treated him as though he was still the emperor and those who were allowed to visit him said he still believed he was the Emperor of Ethiopia. * *"The Emperor", Pgs. 162-163.*

Haile Selassie – Last Days of a Dynasty

The Ethiopian Herald reported that Haile Selassie died of circulatory failure on August 28, 1975.There is considerable disagreement over how he died. An article in the Washington Post implies he was strangled. I don't believe his method of death has ever been clearly determined.

**Factual information for the remainder of the book has been taken from an article in Encarta by Dr. Edmond J. Keller. This information is in sections titled "Mengistu Regime" and "Resistance and Revolution".*

From Dynasty to Socialism to Communism to a Federal Democratic Republic

Following the dethronement of Haile Selassie in 1974 Major Mengistu Haile Mariam, as head of the Provisional Military Administrative Council, took over rule of Ethiopia. This council was better known as the Dergue. Late in 1974 the Dergue issued a program to establish a state controlled socialist economy. In turn all agricultural land was nationalized and then distributed – much of it in small plots to individual farmers. The monarchy was abolished and a republic proclaimed.

With the creation of the republic came an increase in political openness. Ethnic groups such as the Oromo, Afars, Somali, and Eritreans increased their demands for more independence and some even questioned the legitimacy of the new republic. They set up guerrilla forces to fight for independence. Democratic elections were not allowed. In place of elections a Politbureau was composed of the most significant political organizations (a selective process for the purpose of co-opting potential opponents).

It soon became clear in 1975 that Mengistu was vying for more power and intended to take over sole control of the Dergue. Evidence of this was indicated when several of the top leaders of the Dergue were killed, many thought, on orders from Mengistu. The civilian left were not pleased with this move by Mengistu, particularly the Ethiopian People's Revolutionary Party (EPRP). At beginning of 1977 they organized a guerrilla force and launched a campaign to defeat the military forces of Mengistu. This force was known as the "White Terror" and Mengistu's military force was known as the "Red Terror." Mengistu recruited peasants, workers, and public officials, as additional support for the military to oust the enemies of the revolution. An estimated 100,000 or more of these so called enemies of the revolution were killed by Mengistu's Red Forces during 1977 to 1978.

Relations between the United States and Mengistu over human rights violations led to the break up between the two parties and the U.S. withdrew military aid to Ethiopia. This weakened Mengistu's military. It enabled his opponents to take over vast amounts of territory and to destabilize the cities. By 1977 the Eritrean People's Liberation Front (EPLF) controlled most of the territory in that province, and the Tigray People's Liberation Front (TPLF) – supported by the EPLF had gained control of significant amounts of territory in Tigray. To add to Mengistu's problems, the Somalia's had completely routed the Ethiopian army in the Ogaden region.

By early 1978, Mengistu managed to work out a deal with the Russian and Cuban Communist for military assistance that enabled him to regain most of the lost territory. In 1984 Mengistu attempted to gain popular support for his regime. Toward this goal he created the Worker's Party of Ethiopia (WPE), a Marxist-Leninist form of party. In 1987 he organized a new constitution along the lines of the Russian Marxist-Leninist system of government. The new constitution abolished the Dergue but left Mengistu and former Dergue members in control. Mengistu was elected president of Ethiopia.

In spite of the new constitution, the Mengistu government was still opposed by many of the guerrilla groups. They had to go underground when the Dergue had been able to get military assistance from the Russians and Cubans back in 1978. In late 1980s the Mengistu led government had lost the support of the Russians. The attacks of these guerrilla groups plus the loss of Russian support forced Mengistu to call for unconditional peace talks with the Eritrean People's Liberation Front (EPLF) and later with the Ethiopian People's Revolutionary Democratic Front (EPRDF), and the Tigre People's Liberation Front. While these talks were underway the guerrilla forces continued to attack and gain more territory. The port city of Massawa was taken by the EPLF. Later Addis Ababa was surrounded by the EPRDF and taken. Eritrea was lost, Mengistu fled the country and was granted asylum in Zimbabwe, where he still resides.

I have made no attempt to study Ethiopia under the rule of Mengistu. It was a form of communism that in one way or another tried to organize the peasants into cooperatives controlled by the central government. In a way, it seemed a device to substitute communist control for empirical control. Needles to say it failed.

A transitional government was set up by Meles Zenawi in Addis Ababa and EPLF did the same in Eritrea. Eritrea held a referendum in 1993 and declared its independence. Ethiopia recognized the new Eritrean government. In June of 1984 Ethiopian voters elected representatives to a Constituent Assembly and the EPRDF won 484 out of 547 seats. In August of 1995 Meles Zenawi, who headed the EPRDF, was elected by the new legislature as the first prime minister of the newly created Federal Democratic Republic of Ethiopia. He was reelected in October of 2000.

One might think that Ethiopia would finally settle down and live in peace for awhile. Meles Zenawi has proven to be a good prime minister, but Ethiopia seems to thrive on disputes and uses military force to settle the disputes. Aside from Eritrea the Oromo (Galla another name for Oromo) and the Somali have given Ethiopia the most trouble. When we lived in Ethiopia from 1972-74, a guerrilla style conflict was underway between Somali and Ethiopia. At the same time the Eritrean's were trying to gain their independence from Ethiopia. This independence was Ethiopia's award for having been on the winning side in WWII. Eritrea however, never gave up the fight and is now independent, a big loss to Ethiopia as Eritrea now has the important ports of Massawa and Assab, formally controlled by Ethiopia.

All throughout the history of Ethiopia – from the 1600s on – the Galla, or as they prefer to be called the Oromo, have given Ethiopia trouble. Some of this may be attributed to the fact that the Amhara look down on the Oromo because of cultural differences, in dress and physical features. Also most are nomadic and adhere to animist religion. The Oromo outnumber the Amhara, and believe that they should be independent. They also occupy the most productive land and produce much of the coffee that is exported, Ethiopia's most important export.

In mid 1998, a serious clash between Ethiopia and Eritrea broke out along the border between the two countries. Both countries accused the other of seizing its territory. It is noted that the border had not been precisely delineated when Eritrea became independent from Ethiopia in 1993. The latest available information is from the World Fact Book in 2007. It states that in 2002 an Eritrea-Ethiopia Boundary Commission was formed to determine a line that would be agreed to by both countries. Such a line was detailed in November 2006, but neither country responded to the line. In addition to the Boundary Commission – a peace keeping mission – has monitored a 25km wide temporary security zone between the two countries since 2000. This zone has been largely ignored by the rival clans in this area.

As of the present time, Ethiopia is a landlocked country. In my opinion it will not give up the idea of retaking Eritrea at some point. An alternative to Ethiopia is to route Somalia and use Mogadishu as a port. According to the World Fact Book this is exactly what it did in January of 2007. Quoting: *"Ethiopian forces invaded southern Somalia and routed Islamist Courts from Mogadishu…Somaliland secessionist provide port facilities in Berbera and trade ties to landlocked Ethiopia"*.

Ethiopia has recently (in 2009) pulled out of Somalia. This may be related to the unstable conditions that presently exist in Somalia. It has no government, and has not had one in about a decade. Based on recent news reports one might conclude Somalia pirates control the country. In any event there is no agreement by Ethiopia and Eritrea over the boundary line. It is my belief that Ethiopia will eventually gain at least access to the port of Massawa that now belongs to Eritrea.

Ethiopia has a population of just over 85,000,000 and is nearly twice the size of Texas. There is a significant difference in the density of population per square mile. Ethiopia has over twice as many as Texas. More birth control seems to be in order. Slightly over 46 percent of its population is under fifteen years of age and just above fifty one percent are between fifteen and sixty four years of age. Less than three percent of the population is over sixty-four years old Ethiopia has a young population. The median age is 16.9 years. Live expectancy at birth is 55.41 years, which is low compared with that in U.S. of about 76.

Ethiopia's constitution now provides for a president and a prime minister. The president is Girma Woldegiorgis and prime minister is Meles Zenawi. Also the constitution provides for the government to own all the agricultural land and to lease it to farmers on a long term basis. This is an improvement over having a dictator with complete control of the land, but agricultural conditions will never be satisfactory until the land is owned by those who cultivate it. Best of all, Ethiopia can now elect a new head of government on a democratic basis without having a war to pick the winner.

Latest News on Ethiopian Development

I checked the web one last time for the latest information on Ethiopia and found some encouraging news on the development situation. It seems that former President Clinton is taking the lead in tackling the HIV problem in Ethiopia, and other non-government organizations (NGOs) are helping to bring about change in that country.

Tourism

While agriculture is still the major enterprise in Ethiopia, tourism can also become a very important enterprise for Ethiopia. It will first have to develop a comprehensive tourist plan to improve its tourist infrastructure. This would include the building of more hotels and other such facilities, upgrade tourist companies, train guides, build roads, and improve its tourist advertisement. Package and sell tourism that will make a trip to Ethiopia enjoyable and is a must for the most discerning traveler. Of course, a country free of major discord, riots and rebellions is a must. Today with all the pirating underway in neighboring Somalia waters, most tourists will stay away from that part of the world. However, the day can come when the beauty, charm, mystique and ancient historical sites and uniqueness will prevail.

Glimmer of Hope in Ethiopia

A Texas-based organization called A Glimmer of Hope exemplifies the Clinton Global Initiative's (CGI) mandate to turn ideas into action. The organization has fulfilled two commitments to the CGI since 2006 by issuing $2.25 million in microloans to more than 6,000 rural Ethiopians. Prominent supporters of those commitments included:

- The Michael & Susan Dell Foundation
- Whole Planet Foundation (a Whole Foods Market foundation)

Phillip Berber's report about the impact of these loans on some of the poorest people in the world was well received by the CGI members in attendance. CGI's membership comprises over 1,000 of the most influential people in the world; this year's CGI was officially opened by US President Barack Obama on Tuesday.

Latest News on Ethiopian Development

"We have created an efficient and effective way of giving the rural poor a way to make money and lift themselves out of poverty," Berber said. *"Our 2009 commitment will give others an opportunity to piggy-back the work we have already done and have 100% of their money get to the people who need it."*

Berber believes this commitment will allow A Glimmer of Hope to significantly expand the work begun by its first two commitments; $500,000 has already been pledged towards this new initiative.

Just eight years after entering the International Aid arena, Berber has lead his Austin based foundation to national recognition. It underscores Berber's entrepreneurial talents which were originally recognized when he founded CyBerCorp and sold it after five years to Charles Schwab for $488 million – it was one of the biggest success stories of the dot.com era.

After the sale of CyBerCorp, Berber joined his wife Donna at A Glimmer of Hope, the organization she founded to alleviate extreme poverty in Ethiopia. He was convinced that the lessons learned during his business career could be applied to International Aid and Development. He was right again and the organization's investment in Ethiopia has increased as donors have learned of its unique 100% promise.

Since 2001, A Glimmer of Hope has completed:

- 3,500 water projects
- 345 education projects
- 170 health projects
- The rehabilitation of a regional hospital

These efforts have directly and indirectly reached more than 2½ million people with the majority of direct beneficiaries being women and girls, all for an investment of around $35 million.

Though cutting-edge in its approach A Glimmer of Hope has managed to catch the eye of a leading "traditionalist." Tibor Nagy spent over 23 years in the Foreign Service in Africa serving twice as Ambassador; more recently, he served as an advisor to the Obama presidential campaign.

In the Foreign Service Journal, Nagy wrote A Glimmer of Hope's approach was resulting in "dramatic positive outcomes." He has also stated the US government should partner more with emerging NGOs such as A Glimmer of Hope and that the organization's highly integrated model was "the silver bullet for Africa."

Aloha Ethiopia...
(Fairwell to Thee)

Index

Index

Index

Bibliography

Church Committee (1979) *"The Church of Ethiopia"*, Addis Ababa

Doresse, Jean (1959) *"Ethiopia-Ancient Cities And Temples"*, New York & Great Britain

Hancock, Graham (1992) *"The Sign And The Seal"* New York, New York

Hay, Stuart Munro (2002) *"Ethiopia The Unknown Land"*, L. BE .Tauris, London

Hess, Robert L. (1970) *"Ethiopia-The Modernization Of Autocracy"*, New York

Johanson, Donald & Maitland, Edey (1981) *"Lucy"*, New York

Kapuscinski, Ryszard (1983) *"The Emperor"*, Random House, USA

Keller, Edmond J. (1988) *"Revolutionary Ethiopia"*, Indiana University Press, Bloomington and Indianapolis, USA

Last, Geoffrey And Pankhurst (1972), *"A History of Ethiopia in Pictures"*, Oxford University Press, Ely House , London England

Pankhurst, Richard (1992) *"A Social History of Ethiopia"*, The Red Sea Press, Trenton , NJ, USA

Phillipson, David W. (1998) *"Ancient Ethiopia"* The British Museum Press, London, England

Victor Rouche Marquette "Ethiopie", 113, Rue de Paris Boulogne